THE HISTORY OF OLYMPIC SWIMMING, VOLUME I, 1896-1936.

USA Swimming
An imprint of the USA Swimming Press

www.usaswimming.org

Library of Congress Cataloging-in-Publication Data

Daland, Peter.

The History of Olympic Swimming, Volume 1, 1896-1936

ISBN 978-0-615-21779-6
ISBN 978-0-615-26266-6

1. Swimming. 2. Olympic Games, History of   I. Title

First edition: January 2009

10 9 8 7 6 5 4 3 2 1

CONTENTS

Acknowledgements i

Introduction 1

1896   Athens, Greece.. 4

1900   Paris, France.. 7

1904   St. Louis, USA 14

1906   Athens, Greece (Interim Games).. 21

1908   London, Great Britain... 25

1912   Stockholm, Sweden.. 35

1916   Canceled: World War I.. 48

1920   Antwerp, Belgium 49

1924   Paris, France.. 62

1928   Amsterdam, The Netherlands 80

1932   Los Angeles, USA.. 97

1936   Berlin, Germany.. 115

Profiles of Olympians, 1896 – 1936 136

FINA Officers, 1908 – 1936 177

Country Abbreviations.. 178

ACKNOWLEDGEMENTS

The following publishers and authors were kind enough to allow me to use photographs and/or insights from their books:

Norbert Adam "Schwimmania 1899-1999" Verband Osterreicher Schwimvereine, Braunhobergasse, 21/66/2, 1110 Wien, Austria 1999.

"Australian Swimming Celebrating 90 Years", Australian Swimming Inc., Unit. 12, 7Beissel St., Belconnen
Act,   PO Box 32862617 Belconnen Act, Australia.

Baku, Jeno, "Uszosport Almanach 1882-1990/ Hungarian Swimming Federation, Arpad Fej3edelemUtja 8, 1023, Budapest, Hungary.

Baku, Jeno and Serenyi, Peter "Hetvenot ev", Hungarian Swimming Federation, Arpad Fej3edelemUtja 8, 1023, Budapest, Hungary.

Pat Besford "Encyclopedia of Swimming", Robt. Hale & Co., 63 Old Bromton Rd., London SW, Great Britain

Alan Clarkson, "Lanes of Gold", Lester Townsend Publishing Ltd, New South Wales, Australia.

Dansk Svommeunion Fantastiske 100 ar 1907-2007" Book, Ryttergaardsvej 1182, 3528 Farum, Denmark

"75 JahreDeutscher Schwimm Verband 1886-1961".

Yiannis Giannouris, Vouliagmeni, Greece

"100 Jahre Deutscher Schwimm Verband". Karl-Adolph Scherer, Editor

Shingi Higastijima "The Super Swimmers".

Japanese Swimming Federation "History of Japanese Swimming"

"Historiska Simtag 100 Ar" Editors Bosse Alm and Sven von Holst.

Jack Kelso "History of Swimming Competition in Canada".

Joachin Morera," History of Spanish Swimming".

"Natation: 100 Years of French Swimming".

Francois Oppenheim, "Histoire de la Natation"

"Simsport", magazine of the Swedish Swimming Federation.

"Swimming Times," magazine of the ASA, England.

Dr. David Wallechinsky Editor of "The Complete Book of Olympics" Aurum Press Ltd,25 Bedford Ave, London WC1B 3AT, Great Britain.

"The VIII Olympiad, Paris 1924" by Ellen Phillips, World Sport Research & Publications, Inc, 1424 North Highland Ave, Los Angeles, CA 90028.

I would also like to thank the following individuals, many of them close friends, for the assistance they rendered me in researching and writing this book:

Katia Bonjour, Olympic Museum Lausanne, Switzerland.

Forbes Carlile, Ryde, NSW, Australia

Wendy Coles, ASA Loughborough, England.

Cecil Colwin, Ottawa, Canada

Claude Fouquet, Director of La Federation Française de Natation.

Bob Ingram, Senior Editor at *Swimming World*, who copyedited the second draft of this book with his usual diligence and attention to detail

Bob Kiphuth, Head Swimming Coach Yale University and coach of four USA Olympic Teams.

*Dr. William Mallon Olympic Swimming Histories 1896-1920, 303 Southerland Court, Durham, NC 27712, USA

Evelyn Mooseman, Olympic Museum Lausanne, SUI.

Dr. Ivonne Schmid, International Swimming Hall of Fame.

Albert Schoenfield, now deceased, who served as publisher and editor of *Swimming World and Junior Swimmer* from 1960 to 1978

Dr. Heinz Siegel, former Director of the archives of the German Swimming Federation.

Nick Thierry, head of *Swim News*, international magazine and web site from Canada.

Bodo Ungerrechts, Director of swimming archives of the German Swimming Federation.

Bruce Wigo, Executive Director of the International Swimming Hall of Fame.

Chuck Wielgus, Executive Director of USA Swimming, who saw early on the value of this book and offered USA Swimming as Publisher

Finally, I owe a special debt of gratitude to Dr. Phil Whitten, friend and colleague, longtime editor of *Swimming World* magazine, and currently the Executive Director of the College Swimming Coaches Association of America. Phil served as editor, rewriter, photo editor, production manager, copy editor, and fact-checker. His encouragement and diligence helped make this book a reality.

THE HISTORY OF OLYMPIC SWIMMING

1896 - 1936

INTRODUCTION

For many years I have been unable to find a complete and detailed history of either world or Olympic swimming reaching back into the 19th century. Since I was greatly interested in both subjects, this was a surprise and a great disappointment to me. Many excellent volumes have appeared about learning to swim, how to improve stroke technique, land training, weight training, aerobic water work, sprint training, etc., but almost nothing about the history and progress of the great people in our sport — who they were and what they accomplished in their years in swimming.

Since most of the champions from the past are unknown today — even in their own countries — it was clear to me that there was a great need for this gap to be filled as soon as possible. Since a comprehensive history of Olympic swimming obviously was needed, I determined – not without a great deal of trepidation — to attempt this huge task.

After I had written more than half of this volume, I decided to finish it with the 1936 Games in Berlin, the Games at which Adolf Hitler planned to showcase the superiority of the "Aryan race." My decision to end this volume with the Berlin Games, however, had nothing to do with politics.

World War II led to the cancellation of the Games scheduled for 1940 and 1944. So it was not until 1948 -- 12 years after Berlin -- that the Olympic Games resumed. Volume II of this history will cover the postwar period from 1948 - 1964. Volume III will treat the three Olympiads from 1968 to 1976. It was in Mexico City in 1968 that a full program was installed for both sexes with the addition of five events for men and six for women, raising the grand total for both sexes from 18 to 29.

Volumes IV through VI will cover three Olympiads each, with the sixth volume concluding with the London Game of 2012.

PRELUDE

The sport of competition swimming — known more simply as swimming – has been an important segment of the modern Olympic Games since their inception in 1896. Over the past century, this sport has developed and expanded enormously from a rather basic passage through water to the sophisticated events that are held worldwide today.

THE RACING STROKES

During this time, the racing strokes underwent a great deal of evolution so that today's elegant competitive strokes bear only a superficial resemblance to the movements from which they evolved. Current day freestyle or crawl has developed from the 19th century sidestroke to single overarm to double overarm sidestroke to the trudgen stroke into our current styles of two-beat, four-beat and six-beat kick crawl. All of this took place in less than 15 years, roughly between 1895 and 1910.

Breaststroke, which has been used for more than 2,000 years, has undergone several drastic changes since the mid-1930s when the above-water arm action was introduced. The use of this innovation became so widespread that in 1952, FINA (Federation Internationale de Natation Amateur), swimming's international governing body, felt obliged to divide this stroke into two separate styles: breaststroke and butterfly. The first of these was the old orthodox technique with no overarm action permitted. The new style, butterfly, consisted of simultaneous overarm action with a legs-together dolphin kick.

In response to this drastic division, many swimmers resorted to underwater swimming for breaststroke. In 1956, FINA put a one-stroke limit on all underwater movement to force swimmers to return to the old surface style.

Butterfly was received with enthusiasm almost everywhere, resulting in rapid progress worldwide. At first, it was considered by many to be too difficult to perform for events over 100 meters even though the FINA distances were 100 and 200 meters, and the men's Olympic event for 1956 was 200 meters. However, determination and innovation soon triumphed to produce vast numbers of men and women who mastered this new style at the longer distance.

Throughout the nineteenth century and into the first decade of the twentieth, backstroke was nothing more than an upside-down breaststroke, which eventually came to be known as elementary backstroke. Then, alternate arm action and back flutter-kicking were introduced just before World War I, completely changing the style and speed of dorsal swimming.

THE OLYMPIC SWIMMING PROGRAM

The Olympic program of the first modern Games in 1896 was, indeed, modest. It consisted of four events for men only: 100 meters freestyle, 500 meters freestyle and 1200 meters freestyle plus 100 meters freestyle for Greek sailors. These four races were held without preliminaries during part of one morning. In the next two Games — Paris (1900) and St. Louis (1904) — the program varied greatly at the whim of the organizing committees, before a standard set of events and procedures was set up in London in 1908 with six events for men only. They were: the 100 meter freestyle, 400 meter freestyle, 1500 meter freestyle, 100 meter backstroke, 200 meter breaststroke and 4 x 200 meter freestyle relay. With the exceptions of Stockholm (1912) and Antwerp (1920), this program held firm until 1956. In both 1912 and 1920, a 400 meter breaststroke was added.

Women's Olympic swimming began in 1912 with the 100 meter freestyle and 4 x 100 meter freestyle relay. In 1920, a 300 meter freestyle swim was added before the pre-1956 events were established in 1924: 100 meter freestyle, 400 meter freestyle, 100 meter backstroke, 200 meter breaststroke and 4 x 100 meter freestyle relay. This program remained unchanged through 1952.

In 1956 (Melbourne), the 200 meter butterfly for men and 100 meter butterfly for women were added to the Olympic program following FINA's 1952 decision to separate breaststroke into two separate styles. Four years later in Rome, 4 x 100 meter medley relays were added for both men and women. Then in Tokyo (1964), the men's backstroke was lengthened to 200 meters, the 4 x 100 meter freestyle relay was added and both sexes gained a 400 meter individual medley event.

OLYMPIC FACILITIES

The development of racing facilities has been equally dramatic over this same period. The first three Games were held, respectively, in the rough, salty, tidal water of the Aegean Sea; the cloudy, swiftly-flowing Seine River; and the man-made "Lifesaving Lake" in St. Louis, Missouri. The water in each of these primitive courses was extremely cold and unclear. No lane lines or proper turning facilities were available in those Olympics.

The lot of the spectator was hardly better than that of the competitor at these early Games. For most, it was a question of standing in crowded areas on the side or end of the course. There were no aquatic stadia with thousands of seats.

In the pre-1908 Olympic competition, most of the world's best swimmers were not entered for various reasons: lack of interest in the Games, lack of funds, politics, etc. Therefore these meetings did not decide who the true champions were, but rather, who were the best of those present in the offered events.

THE NON OLYMPIC EVENTS

Olympic events that were restricted to entries from the host country have been omitted because they do not qualify as part of Olympic swimming history. When Olympic medals are counted, these events should not be considered. Thus, the 1896 race for Greek sailors and the 1904 freestyle relay – limited to teams from the USA – are not included because only swimmers from the host country were allowed to compete.

1896: ATHENS, GREECE
(Open Salt Water, Bay of Zea)

Start of the 500-meter freestyle at the first Modern Olympic Games in 1896. Twenty-six of the 31 entrants in the event withdrew, due to extremely rough conditions in the Bay of Zea near Athens.

Following the 1894 meeting of the International Athletic Congress, it was decided to stage the first Modern Olympic Games in and around Athens, Greece two years later. In 1896, the Games were revived with much pomp and ceremony by the Greek royal family and by many enthusiasts of international amateur sports, led by Baron de Coubertin of France. Swimming was chosen as one of the competitions to be held, with a program of four events for men on the 11th of April in the Olympic year.

These aquatic events were staged in the Aegean Sea and the Bay of Zea, part of the port of Piraeus. The first two races, the open 100 meter freestyle and the 100 meter freestyle for sailors of the Greek Navy, were swum in the protected waters of the Bay itself. Starting from the water, the contestants raced to a finish flag near the shore.

100 Meter Freestyle (Open): Alfred Hajos (HUN), born Guttmann, won this event by a meter over Eustathios Khoraphas (GRE) with Otto Herschmann (AUT) only centimeters behind. In this first event, there were 13 entries representing five nations competing in cold salt water —55° F. or 13° C. — much lower than today's required racing temperature of 25°-28° C., or 77°-82° F.

500 Meter Freestyle: Paul Neumann (AUT) captured this intermediate distance in 8:12.6 over two Greeks, Antonios Pepanos and Khoraphas. Twenty-six others scratched from the race, which started in the rough and cold Aegean Sea outside the entrance to the Bay. Sometime after these Games, Neumann moved to Chicago, where he won USA championships and practiced medicine.

In 1896, Alfred Hajos (HUN) won the first event swum in the modern Olympic Games: the 100-meter freestyle. He added a second gold medal in the 1200-meter freestyle, swum in the frigid, storm-tossed waters of the Bay of Zea near Athens.

1200 Meter Freestyle: Resting during the 500 meter freestyle Hajos came back for a big win in this distance event, clocking 18:22.2, to defeat eight other swimmers, mostly Greek. Starting from the sides of boats in the open sea, the competitors battled frigid (55° F) water and huge, 12-foot waves, until they reached the protected bay and the finish flag. Afterward, Hajos stated that under the terrible racing conditions, he was swimming more for his life than for an Olympic gold medal. In later years, this double Olympic winner became a famous architect in his native Budapest. His work included the design of the famous 33-1/3 meter pool on Margaret Island in the Danube River at Budapest.

Unfortunately, most of the best swimmers in the world did not compete in these inaugural Games in Greece. Australia, Great Britain and Germany — the top aquatic countries of this period — were wholly unrepresented in swimming at Athens.

Dr. Paul Neumann, of Austria, captured the 500-meter freestyle in a race in which 26 of the 29 entrants scratched due to the stormy seas.

1896 OLYMPIC SWIMMING RESULTS
ATHENS, GREECE
BAY OF ZEA (PIRAEUS)
OPEN WATER STRAIGHTAWAY

Men's 100 Meter Freestyle: **Final**
1) Alfred Hajos   (HUN)   o1:22.2
2) Eustathios Khoraphas   (GRE)   1:23.0
3) Otto Herschmann   (AUT)   1:23.0
   Aminos   (GRE)
   Gardner Williams   (USA)   No Time
   Alexandros Khrisafos   (GRE)   No Time

Men's 500 meter Freestyle: **Final**
1) Paul Neumann   (AUT)   o8:12.6
2) Antonios Pepanos   (GRE)   9:57.6
3) Eustathios Khoraphas   (GRE)   No Time

Men's 1200 Meter Freestyle: **Final**
1) Alfred Hajos   (HUN)   o18:22.2
2) Ioannis Andreou   (GRE)   21:03.4
3) Eustathios Khoraphas   (GRE)   No time
   Katravas   (GRE)
   Gardner Williams   (USA)
   Paul Neumann   (AUT)   DNF

o Olympic Record

1896 Men's Olympic Swimming Medals

	Gold	Total
Hungary	2	2
Austria	1	2
Greece	0	5

1900: Paris, France
(100 Meter Course in the Seine River)
At Asnières

Divers perform at Asnieres on the Seine River in Paris, site of the aquatic competition at the 1900 Olympic Games. Some of the boats used as obstacles in the 200-meter obstacle course race are still in place.

The second Olympics of the modern era were awarded to Paris, France, for 1900 in spite of some pressure to return them to Athens. Unfortunately, these Games were badly overshadowed by the magnificent Paris International Exposition of that same year. Over the protest of Baron de Coubertin, president of the International Olympic Committee (IOC), the Games were relegated to "side-show" status. To generate more public interest, some sports, including swimming, were billed as World Championships.

Despite being eclipsed by the World Fair, the size and quality of the Games grew impressively from their modest beginnings in Greece four years earlier. Swimming expanded its program from three to seven events. The number of nations entered grew from four to 12 with the number of swimmers increasing greatly. The major absentees included most of the Australian champions plus the best from the United States and Sweden.

The racing course for swimming, alleged to have been 100 meters in length, was set between two floating platforms in the Seine River near Asnières. Despite the strong current, the dark water and the primitive conditions for starting and turning, this facility was acclaimed by the French press as the "Magnificent Pool of Asnières." Perhaps part of this praise was due to the unbelievable performances of the

7

swimmers. In fact, the times were so fast that most experts agree that the course must have been shorter than 100 meters or that the competitors swam downstream. On average, the medal winners were 15 percent faster than they were before or after this meet.

Little Freddie Lane (AUS) from Sydney and strongman John Jarvis (GBR) from Leicester in England, were the big stars of these swimming events with two victories each. Of the three other finals, two were won by Germans and one by a Frenchman.

Freddie Lane (AUS) won two events at the Paris Games of 1900: the 200-meter freestyle and the 200-meter obstacle. Lane's impossibly fast winning time in the 200 free came with an assist from the current in the Seine River.

200 Meter Freestyle: Lane, a small, slender champion from the East Sydney Swim Club, easily swam away from his English and continental rivals to capture this race in the impossible time of 2:25.2. This clocking, twenty seconds under his lifetime best, was not bettered over the long course for 17 years. Far behind, Zoltan Halmay (HUN) beat Karl Ruberl (AUT) for second. Curiously, Ruberl had qualified first in the heats with the unbelievable time of 2:22.6 while Lane won his heat with a modest 2:59.0 for only the 10th fastest preliminary time.

200 Meter Obstacle Swim: In a wild scramble over and under a set of boats and other barriers, Lane captured this title by less than two seconds over Austrian veteran Otto Wahle. Far behind was Peter Kemp (GBR), some four seconds ahead of Karl Ruberl (AUT). Both Wahle and Ruberl later moved to New York, where they swam for the New York Athletic Club.

1000 Meter Freestyle: Barrel-chested John Jarvis, a multiple-champion distance swimmer from England, captured the 1000 meter freestyle with his powerful overarm sidestroke by more than a minute in 13:40.2. This world record time was more than two minutes faster than he had ever swum before and was not bettered until 1923. Wahle (AUT) finished a distant second, ahead of, Zoltan Halmay (HUN) and Max Hainle (GER).

4000 Meter Freestyle: Taking full advantage of the current in the Seine River, Jarvis forged an even greater margin of victory in the longer 4,000 meter race. His time – an astonishing 58:24 — was more than 10 minutes ahead of Halmay and Louis Martin (FRA). In both events the long and relaxed overarm sidestroke produced victory for the powerful Englishman.

Using the sidestroke, Britain's barrel-chested John Jarvis took both distance events in Paris – the 1,000 and 4,000-meter freestyle.

200 Meter Backstroke: Ernst Hoppenberg, from the Bremer Swim Club in Germany, defeated Karl Ruberl (AUT, WSK) in the 200 meter backstroke by the huge margin of nine seconds with Johannes Drost (NED, RZC) back another five seconds. The winner's time of 2:47.0 was not bettered by anyone for over twenty years in spite of the slow elementary backstroke style of that period.

Ernst Hoppenberg, Germany, won the 200-meter back-stroke in 2:47.0 – more than nine seconds ahead of the second-place finisher. His time, assisted by the river current, was not bettered for more than two decades. He picked up a second gold in the 200-meter team swim.

Underwater Swim: Charles de Vendeville (FRA) beat countryman Andre Six in a very close contest in an event also known as the "Plunge for Distance." The scores were awarded on a point system based on time and distance under the surface.

200 Meter Team Event: Germany outswam four French teams in this 200 meter event of five man teams, scored like cross country. It was curious that France entered several club teams instead of a national team. Even so, the Germans still would have won with their faster swimmers.

Men's 200 Meter Freestyle:

			Semi-Final		Final
1) Fred Lane	(AUS)		2:59.0	III	2:25.2
2) Zoltan Halmay	(HUN)		2:38.0	II	2:31.4
3) Karl Ruberl	(AUT)		o2:22.6	V	2:32.0
4 Robert Crawshaw	(GBR)		2:40.0	I	2:45.6
5 Maurice Hochepied	(FRA)		2:48.0	V	2:53.0
6 F.Stapleton	(GBR)		2:47.0	V	2:55.0
Jules Clevenot	(FRA)		3:05.0	IV	2:56.2
Julius Frey	(GER)		2:50.4	I	2:58.2
Louis Martin	(FRA)		2:47.4	V	No Time
Otto Wahle	(AUT)		2:35.6		
Peter Kemp	(GBR)		2:51.0		
Erik Eriksson	(SWE)		3:05.8		
Herman Alex de Bij	(NED)		3:10.4		
Feret	(FRA)		3:12.2		
Tartara	(FRA)		3:13.0		
Victor Cadet	(FRA)		3:24.0		
Bussetti	(ITA)		3:35.0		
Fred Henschel	(USA)		3:42.0		
Texier	(FRA)		3:47.0		
Peyrusson	(FRA)		3:47.6		
Adam	(FRA)		4:28.0		
N. Forregger	(USA)		4:32.0		
Ronaux	(FRA)		4:36.4		
Leaute	(FRA)		4:39.4		
Pujol (FRA)			DNF		

Men's 1000 Meter Freestyle:

		Semifinal		Final
1) John Jarvis	(GBR)	14:28.6	I	o13:40.2
2) Otto Wahle	(AUT)	15:27.0	III	14:53.6
3) Zoltan Halmay	(HUN)	14:52.0	III	15:16.0
4 Max Hainle	(GER)	15:54.0	III	15:22.0
5 Louis Martin	(FRA)	16:58.0	IV	16:30.4
6 Jean Levilleux	(FRA)	17:09.6	II	16:53.2
Thomas Burgess	(GBR)	16:54.0	IV	
Maurice Hochepied	(FRA)	17:13.2	I	
Verbeke	(FRA)	17:18.0	II	
Erik Eriksson	(SWE)	17:41.2	I	
Fumouze	(FRA)	18:00.0	I	
Desire Merchez	(FRA)	18:17.2	III	
Texier	(FRA)	21:33.0	IV	
Lue	(FRA)	24:15.0	II	
Souchu	(FRA)	25:52.0	II	

Men's 4000 Meter Freestyle:		Semi-Final		Final
1) John Jarvis	(GBR)	1:01:48.4I		o58:24.0
2) Zoltan Halmay	(HUN)	1:11:33.4II		1:08:55.4
3) Louis Martin	(FRA)	1:22:29.6I		1:13:08.4
4 Thomas Burgess	(GBR)	1:15:04.8I		1:15:07.6
5 Eduard Meijer	(NED)	1:17:55.4II		1:16:37.2
6 Fabio Mainoni	(ITA)	1:25:16.6III		1:26:32.2
7 E.Martin	(FRA)	1:28:32.6III		1:26:32.2
Anderle	(AUT)	1:26:25.6I		DNF
William Henry	(GBR)	1:22:58.4II		DNF
Texier	(FRA)	1:31:02.8II		
Louis Laufray	(FRA)	1:35:03.2III		
Kobierski	(FRA)	1:37:10.4II		
Legarde	(FRA)	1:38:31.8I		
Mortier	(FRA)	1:40:16.8III		
Lue	(FRA)	1:46:40.4II		
De Romand	(FRA)	1:50:36.4I		
Fumouze	(FRA)	2:02:27.oI		
Hermand	(BEL)	DNF		
Jean Levillieux	(FRA)	DNF		
Gallais	(FRA)	DNF		
L. Baudoin	(FRA)	DNF		
Landrich	(FRA)	DNF		
Gelle (FRA)	DNF			
Heyberger	(FRA)	DNF		
Regnault	(FRA)	DNF		
Jules Clevenor	(FRA)	DNF		
E. T. Jones	(GBR)	DNF		
Loppe	(FRA)	DNF		
Vallee(FRA)	DNF			

Men's 200 Meter Backstroke:		Semi-Final		Final
1) Ernst Hoppenberg	(GER)	2:54.4	I	o2:47.0
2) Karl Ruberl	(AUT)	2:56.0	III	2:56.0
3) Johannes Drost	(NED)	3:10.2	III	3:01.0
4 Johannes Bleomen	(NED)	3:09.2	II	3:02.2
5 Thomas Burgess	(GBR)	2:50.4	I	3:12.6
6 de Romand	(FRA)	3:56.6	II	3:38.0
7 Bussetti	(ITA)	3:50.4	I	3:45.0
8 Erik Eriksson	(SWE)	4:05.4	III	3:56.4
Jean Levillieux	(FRA)	3:10.2	III	DNF
Robert Crawshaw	(GBR)	3:15.0	I	DNF
Lue	(FRA)	4:10.0		
Peyrusson	(FRA)	4:15.6		
Chevrand	(FRA)	4:42.0		
Texier	(FRA)	4:49.0		
Lapostelet	(FRA)	4:34.6		
Fumouze	(FRA)	5:17.0		

Men's 200 Meter Obstacle Race:

			Semi-Final		Final
1) Fred Lane	(AUS)	3:04.0	I		o2:38.4
2) Otto Wahle	(AUT)	2:56.0	II		2:40.0
3) Peter Kemp	(GBR)	3:12.0	III		2:47.4
4 Karl Ruberl	(AUT)	3:06.0	I		2:51.2
5 F.Stapleton	(GBR)	3:18.4	I		2:55.0
6 William Henry	(GBR)	3:14.4	II		2:56.0
7 Maurice Hochepied	(FRA)	3:37.2	II		2:58.0
8 Verbecke	(FRA)	3:18.0	II		3:08.4
9 Bertrand	(FRA)	3:28.2	III		3:17.0
10 Louis Marc	(FRA)	3:29.2	I		3:30.6
Victor Hochepied	(FRA)	3:37.2	II		
Fred Hendschel	(USA)	3:45.2	III		

Men's 200 Meter Team Swim:

1) Germany   (E. Hoppenberg 2:35.4, M. Hainle 2:36.0, G. Lexau 2:42.0, H. Luhrsen 2:55.0, H. von Petersdforf DNS)

2) France   PN Lille (J. Tartara 2:48.6, L. Martin 2:51.4, D. Merchez 2:55.4, Jean Levillieux 3:02.0, DNS)

2) France   Tritons Lillois (M. Hochepied 2:53.0, V. Hochepied 2:56.4, Bertrand 3:00.0, Verbecke 3:01.6, M.Cadet 3:18.0)

4) France   Libellule (J. Clevenot 2:45.0, Feret 3:00.4, Gasaigne 3:02.0, Rosier 3:04.4, Pelloy 3:06.0)

Men's Underwater Swim:

		Meters	Time	Score
1) Charles de Vendeville	(FRA)	60.0	1:08.4	188.4
2) Andre Six	(FRA)	60.0	1:05.4	185.4
3) Peder Lykkeberg	(DEN)	28.5	1:30.0	147.0
De Romand	(FRA)	47.5	50.2	145.2
Tisserand	(FRA)	30.75	48.0	109.5
Hans Aniol	(GER)	36.95	30.0	103.9
Menault	(FRA)	32.5	38.4	103.4
Louis Marc	(FRA)	34.0	32.0	100.0
Peyrusson	(FRA)	31.0	29.6	91.6
Kaisermann	(FRA)	16.1	56.8	88.8
Leclerc	(FRA)	30.0	28.0	88.0
Chevrand	(FRA)	20.0	32.0	72.0
Anderle	(AUT)	23.5	22.4	69.4
Eucher	(FRA)	21.5	23.0	66.0

o Olympic Record

1900 Men's Olympic Swimming Medals

	Gold	Medals
GBR	2	3
AUS	2	2
GER	2	2
FRA	1	4
AUT	0	4
HUN	0	3
DEN	0	1
NED	0	1

1896–1900 Men's Olympic Swimming Medals

	Gold	Medals
HUN	2	5
GBR	2	3
AUS	2	2
GER	2	2
AUT	1	6
FRA	1	4
GRE	0	5
DEN	0	1
NED	0	1

1904: St. Louis, USA
(110 Yard Course in a Lake)

Start of the100-yard freestyle at the Life Saving Lake in St. Louis, site of the 1904 Games. Hungary's Zoltan Halmay won by a touch over the USA's Charlie Daniels in 1:02.8. Halmay also took the 50-yard free.

Following the disappointment of the Paris Games, the International Olympic Committee (IOC) decided to reward the strong overall American participation in the first two Olympics by holding the 1904 Games in Chicago. Unfortunately, President Theodore Roosevelt changed them to St. Louis to accompany the Louisiana Purchase Exposition that was planned for that same city in the summer of 1904. Once again, the public was more interested in the Fair than the Games.

The swimming events were to be held in an artificial pond named "Lifesaving Lake," which was to be created near the middle of town. Because of delays in preparing this facility, the swimming competition was postponed until September 5. The diminished status of the swimming events resulted in almost no foreign entrants.

For this competition, the racing course of 110 yards (100.58 meters) was between a floating pier and floating rafts. Even though such a primitive facility, without lane lines of any sort, would be totally unacceptable by modern standards, it was still vastly superior to the open sea at Athens and the flowing River Seine in Paris.

Because of the small international contingent consisting of precisely seven swimmers from three countries, this meet was also designated as the USA Outdoor National AAU Championships, with the vast majority of the competitors coming from American clubs. There were no entries from the leading swimming nations, Australia and Great Britain.

The missing British and Australian swimmers would have raised the level of Olympic performance significantly if they had competed in St. Louis. The Australians — Richard Cavill, Barney Kieran and Alex Wickham — and the English — John Jarvis, David Billington, Rob Derbyshire, William Call and William Robinson – almost certainly would have dominated these Games.

In their absence, the leading figures in St. Louis were double winners: Zoltan Halmay (HUN) from the MUE Club; Emil Rausch (GER), representing the Poseidon Club in Berlin; and Charles Daniels (USA) of the New York AC. These three swimmers captured all of the freestyle titles.

Zoltan Halmay (HUN), double gold medalist in St. Louis.

50 Yard Freestyle: This shortest of events proved to be the most controversial. Scott Leary (USA) of the Olympic Club led through the heats with an excellent 28.6 to 29.6 by Halmay. In the final, a clear win by the tall Hungarian was negated when the timers clocked both men in 28.2. The officials ordered the final to be reswum. It was, and this time there was absolutely no doubt as Halmay beat Leary 28.0 to 28.6, with the slender Daniels a close third.

100 Yard Freestyle: Halmay qualified nearly a second faster than Daniels in the heats in 1:06.2. In the final, the Hungarian won by a hand over the young New Yorker with Leary in third. Halmay's time of 1:02.8 was excellent in view of the slow course conditions.

Charlie Daniels, the greatest freestyler of his day, won both the 220- and 440-yard freestyle events.

220 Yard Freestyle: Charles Daniels defeated fellow American Francis Gailey from the Olympic Club in a hard-fought race, finishing in 2:44.2 to 2:46.0 for the San Franciscan. German distance champion, Emil Rausch, placed third another ten seconds behind (2:56.0).

440 Yard Freestyle: In the quarter mile final, Daniels forged a margin of victory of nearly six seconds over Gailey, 6:16.2 to 6:22.0. Though well behind the leaders, Austrian Otto Wahle (6:39.0) outswam America's Bud Goodwin of the New York AC for third. Later, Wahle moved to New York, where he coached both Daniels and Goodwin at the New York AC. In 1912 and 1920, he was the Olympic swimming team leader for the USA.

880 Yard Freestyle: Emil Rausch won this event in 13:11.4, twelve seconds ahead of Gailey (13:23.4), with Geza Kiss (HUN) from the MUE Club in third. Absentee Barney Kieran (AUS) had swum more than 1:40 faster than the Olympic champion at the Australian nationals half-a-year earlier.

One Mile Freestyle: Rausch swam away with this longest race, leaving runner-up Kiss over a minute behind, 27:18.2 to 28:28.2, with Gailey a distant third in 28:54.0. Again, the winning time was well behind Kieran's 24:36.2 from the Australian Nationals.

Germany's Emil Rausch was the distance king of the 1904 Games, winning both the half-mile and the mile and placing third in the 220.

100 Yard Backstroke: This first-ever Olympic backstroke event produced a German sweep of all three medals. Walter Brack from Berlin was the winner in 1:16.8. Behind him came Georg Hoffman (1:18.0) of Poseidon Berlin and Georg Zacharias (1:19.6) from Weissensee '96. The AAU had added this event as well as the 440 yard breaststroke to attract European participation. Both events were part of some European meets, but were not contested in the USA at that time.

440 Yard Breaststroke: In this long race, Zacharias outswam Brack by five meters to become the first Olympic breaststroke champion in 7:23.6. Jamison Handy (USA) of the Chicago AA beat Hoffmann for the bronze medal.

The reason for the same swimmers excelling in both backstroke and breaststroke in this period is that, at the time, the backstroke was swum with a style we now call

Georg Zacharias, Germany, won the 440-yard breaststroke and was third in the 100-yard backstroke.

"elementary backstroke," which is nothing more than upside down breaststroke.

The results of the 4 x 50 yard free relay have not been recorded here because this event was held only as a National AAU Championship race. When a German squad tried to enter this team event, they were told that it was only for American clubs.

Olympic Problems after the 1904 Games

After three Olympiads, it had become clear to many who were close to the Games that several changes were needed to bring order out of chaos:

- First, the events needed to be standardized. Through the 1904 Games, not a single event had been held more than once.
- Second, the rules of competition needed to be regularized. In the first three Games, all events had been swum under the regulations of the host nation.
- Third, the conditions of competition needed to be made uniform. This last point became obvious after reviewing the racing conditions of these first three Games: open sea, flowing river and a small lake.
- Finally, if the Games were to survive, never again should they be held under the shadow of another international event, as they had in Paris and St. Louis.

It was clear that an international swimming organization was needed to solve these problems.

1904 OLYMPIC SWIMMING RESULTS
ST. LOUIS, USA
110 YARD COURSE IN LIFESAVING LAKE

Men's 50 Yard Freestyle:		Semi-Final	Final	Reswim
1) Zoltan Halmay	(HUN)	o29.6	o28.2	o28.0
2) Scott Leary	(USA)	o28.6	o28.2	28.6
3) Charles Daniels	(USA)			
4 David Gaul	(USA)			
5 Leo "Bud" Goodwin	(USA)			
6 Raymond Thorne	(USA)			

Men's 100 Yard Freestyle:		Semi-Final	Final
1) Zoltan Halmay	(HUN)	o1:06.2	o1:02.8
2) Charles Daniels	(USA)	1:07.4	
3) Scott Leary	(USA)		
4 David Gaul	(USA)		
5 David Hammond	(USA)		
6 Leo "Bud" Goodwin	(USA)		

220 Yard Freestyle:		Final
1) Charles Daniels	(USA)	o2:44.2
2) Francis Gailey	(USA)	2:46.0
3) Emil Rausch	(GER)	2:56.0
4 Edgar Adams	(USA)	

440 Yard Freestyle:		Final
1) Charles Daniels	(USA)	o6:16.2
2) Francis Gailey	(USA)	6:22.0
3) Otto Wahle	(AUT)	6:39.0
4 Leo "Bud" Goodwin	(USA)	

880 Yard Freestyle:		Final
1) Emil Rausch	(GER)	o13:11.4
2) Francis Gailey	(USA)	13:23.4
3) Geza Kiss	(HUN)	
4 Edgar Adams	(USA)	
5 Otto Wahle	(AUT)	
6 H. Jamison "Jam" Handy	(USA)	

Men's 1 Mile Freestyle:		Final
1) Emil Rausch	(GER)	o27:18.2
2) Geza Kiss	(HUN)	28:28.2
3) Francis Gailey	(USA)	28:54.0

4	Otto Wahle	(AUT)	No Time
	Edgar Adams	(USA)	DNF
	Louis deB. Handley	(USA)	DNF
	John Meyers	(USA)	DNF

Men's 100 Yard Backstroke: Final

1) Walter Brack   (GER)   o1:16.8
2) Georg Hoffmann   (GER)   1:18.0
3) Georg Zacharias   (GER)   1:19.6
4 William Ortwein   (USA)   No Time
   Edwin Swatek   (USA)   No Time
   David Hammond   (USA)   No Time

Men's 440 Yard Breaststroke: Final

1) Georg Zacharias   (GER)   o7:23.6
2) Walter Brack   (GER)   (5 mts behind)
3) Jamison Handy   (USA)
4 Georg Hoffman   (GER)
                     o Olympic Record

1904 Men's Olympic Swimming Medals

	Gold	Medals
GER	4	8
USA	2	11
HUN	2	4
AUT	0	1

1896-1904 Men's Olympic Swimming Medals

	Gold	Medals
GER	6	10
HUN	4	9
USA	2	11
GBR	2	3
AUS	2	2
AUT	1	7
FRA	1	4
GRE	0	5
DEN	0	1
NED	0	1

1906: Athens, Greece (Interim Games)
Open Sea

The second visit to Athens, in 1906, did much to keep the struggling Olympic movement alive. The swimming events were held over a straightaway course in the Aegean Sea off Athens. In spite of the adverse effects of wind, waves, tide, current and cold water, this turned out to be the best international competition up to that time. All of the major swimming nations were represented in these races. Six countries from three continents shared the medals in the four swimming events. Due to the less than ideal conditions the times were mediocre, but the competition was excellent.

Scoring five times in the top three, Great Britain emerged as the biggest winner in these Games. Britain's unlikely distance duo – the diminutive Henry Taylor (Hyde Seal SC) and veteran strong man John Jarvis (Leicester SC) — led the British team with two individual medals each plus a third medal in the relay event.

100 Meter Freestyle: American Charles Daniels from the New York AC reversed the results of the 110 yard freestyle two years earlier in St. Louis, when he won the 100 meter free over Hungarian Zoltan Halmay of the MTK Club by a full body length, 1:13.0 to 1:14.2. Third-place finisher, stocky Cecil Healy of Australia, had swum 1:07.4 in Hamburg, Germany earlier in the year over a 100-meter, salt-water course. Even allowing for the superior conditions in Germany, Healy's time was more than two seconds faster than Kieran's world long course best from 1905.

Charlie Daniels takes his mark in the 100-meter freestyle at the "Interim Games," held in Athens in 1906.

400 Meter Freestyle: The powerful Austrian champion, Otto Scheff, from the Wiener SC, was just able to hold Taylor off in a close battle in this middle distance event, 6:23.8 to 6:24.4. Jarvis took third in 6:27.2. By comparison, at the Australian Championships of that same year, Barney Kieran had swum 5:38.2 a few days before his tragic death at the age of 19.

1600 Meter Freestyle: The story was very different in the metric mile as Taylor easily swam away from teammate Jarvis, 28:28.0 to 30:07.6. Scheff was a remote third in 30:53.4. The famous 1904 winner, Emil Rausch (GER) of the Poseidon Berlin SC), was a distant fifth. The champion was over a minute behind his own English ASA Championship time of 1906 and nearly four minutes slower than R. Healy at the 1906 New South Wales Meet in Sydney.

Britain's distance aces in the early 1900s were beefy John Jarvis (right) and Henry Taylor. In Athens, with Taylor leading, the pair went one-two in the 1600-meter freestyle; two-three behind Austria's Otto Scheff in the 400; and picked up bronze in the 4 x 250-meter freestyle relay.

4 x 250 Meter Freestyle Relay: The Hungarian quartet of Jozsef Onody, Alfred Hajos, Geza Kiss and Zoltan Halmay, gave the Magyars an easy, nearly 24-second victory over Germany, with Britain beating the USA for the bronze in this new relay distance.

Unfortunately no backstroke or breaststroke events were offered at this big inter-Olympic meet. Aside from the masters of these two strokes, very few of the world's best swimmers missed this competition.

1906 INTERIM GAMES SWIMMING RESULTS
ATHENS, GREECE
OPEN WATER IN THE BAY

Men's 100 Meter Freestyle:		Semi-Final	Final
1) Charles Daniels	USA	o1:17.6 I	o1:13.0
2) Zoltan Halmay	HUN	No Time II	1:14.2
3) Cecil Healy	AUS	1:17.8 I	No Time
4 Paul Radmilovic	GBR	No Time II	No Time
5 John Derbyshire	GBR	No Time I	No Time
6 Jozsef Onody	HUN	No Time II	No Time
7 Marquard Schwartz	USA	No Time II	No Time
8 Hjalmar Johansson	SWE	No Time II	No Time
9 Robert Andersson	SWE	No Time I	No Time
Albert Bouguin	FRA	No Time I	
Ludvig Dam	DEN	No Time I	
Harald Julin	SWE	No Time II	
Georg Hoffmann	GER	No Time II	
Mario Albertino	ITA	No Time II	
Vasilios Leontopoulos	GRE	No Time II	
Spiridon Tzetzos	GRE	No Time II	
P. Paraskevopoulos	GRE	No Time I	

400 meter Freestyle:		Final
1) Otto Scheff	AUT	6:23.8
2) Henry Taylor	GBR	6:24.4
3) John Jarvis	GBR	6:27.2
4 Alajos Bruckner	HUN	No Time
5 Paul Radmilovic	GBR	No Time
6 Cecil Healy	AUS	No Time
Zoltan Tobias	HUN	DNF
John H. Derbyshire	GBR	DNF
Vasilos Leontopoulos	GRE	DNF
Konstantinos Kleinias	GRE	DNF
Konstan. Panteleskos	GRE	DNF
Hjalmar Saxtorph	DEN	DNF
Frank Bornamann	USA	DNF

1600 Meter Freestyle:		Final
1) Henry Taylor	GBR	o28:28.0
2) John Jarvis	GBR	30:07.6
3) Otto Scheff	AUT	30:53.4
4 Max Pape	GER	32:34.6
5 Emil Rausch	GER	32:40.6
6 Ernst Bahnmeyer	GER	33:29.4
7 Oskar Schiele	GER	33:52.4
8 Leopold Mayer	AUT	34:41.0
9 Joseph Spencer	USA	34:50.0

10	Simon Orlik	AUT	36:25.0
11	Hjalmar Saxtorph	DEN	38:24.0
	Albert Bouguin	FRA	DNF
	Stanley Cooper	GBR	DNF
	Cecil Healy	AUS	DNF
	Vasilios Leontopoulos	GRE	DNF
	Charles Norilius	SWE	DNF
	Paul Radmilovic	GBR	DNF
	Nils Regnell	SWE	DNF
	Georgios Soulis	GRE	DNF
	Spiridon Tzetzos	GRE	DNF
	Paul Vasseur	FRA	DNF
	Gustaf Wretman	SWE	DNF
	Mario Albertini	ITA	DNF
	Edmund Bernhardt	AUT	DNF

4x250 Meter Freestyle Relay: Final

1) HUN (Onody,Hajos,Kiss,Halmay)   o16:52.4
2) GER (Bahnmeyer,Schiele,Rausch,Pape)   17:16.2
3) GBR (Henry,Derbyshire,Jarvis,Taylor)   No Time
4 USA (Bornamann,Spencer,Schwartz,Daniels)   No Time
5 SWE (Julin,Wretman,Norelius,Regnell)   No Time
    AUT   DNF

o Olympic Record

1908: London, England
(100 Meter Outdoor Pool)

The 4-lane, 100-meter Olympic Pool in the infield of the main Olympic stadium at the 1908 Games in London. No swimming stadium constructed in the century since then has surpassed London's in terms of seating capacity. Cheered by the partisan home crowd, Britain dominated swimming in 1908.

The International Olympic Committee (IOC) originally selected Rome as the site for the 1908 Olympic Games. However, at the 1906 Interim Games it was decided to move the Games to London due to an acute financial crisis in Italy. This shift to the largest population center in the Western world gave to the Olympics the push that was needed as a follow-up to the Interim Games. All the resources of the capital of the mighty British Empire were mobilized for these London Olympics. At that time, the vast group of nations under British rule covered 20 percent of the Earth's surface and included one-fourth of its population. Taking place only a scant six years before the outbreak of the First World War, these Edwardian Games were far greater in every aspect than any previous international sporting event.

In Paris in 1900 and St. Louis in 1904, the Games were eclipsed by gigantic international expositions that pushed the Olympic competitions into the background. By contrast, in 1908, the British organizers put all of their energy and skills into presenting a truly great Olympic Games. For swimming, the combined efforts of the Amateur Swimming Association (ASA) under George Hearn and the Royal Life Saving Society led by Bill Henry were of enormous assistance to the organizers.

The success of the 1908 swimming events was due, in part, to the remarkable venue and facility in which they were held. Under the direction of former British Olympic swimmer, Bill Henry, a four-lane, 100-meter x 15-meter pool was constructed for the aquatic events. This first-ever Olympic pool was placed in the infield of the main Olympic stadium . Installed inside the running track, the pool ranged from 1.2 to 3.7 meters in depth to accommodate the requirements of diving and water polo as well as those of swimming. In the middle of the pool, Henry had installed a collapsible tower for platform diving. This structure was folded up into the pool when aquatic events or practice sessions were not in progress. Unfortunately for all three sports, the unfiltered water was dark and cold.

The aquatic sports had never before been held in the main Olympic stadium — nor have they since 1908. This vast arena was able to accommodate over 60,000 spectators. Since then, swimming has never been able to offer even half of this seating capacity.

For the first time in modern Olympic history, the London Games brought

Charlie Daniels, USA, smiles after winning the 100-meter freestyle with a world record 1:05.6, nipping Hungary's Zoltan Halmay by six-tenths of a second. Daniels also picked up a bronze as a member of the USA's 4x200-m freestyle relay.

together the best swimmers in the world with only two notable exceptions: Cecil Healy from Sydney, Australia and Emil Rausch from Berlin, Germany. The former was unable to raise the funds for the long trip from "Down Under"; the latter swam in the German nationals instead. Healy might well have won the 100 meter free since he swam an incredible 1:03.2 in a salt-water, 110-yard race in Sydney a few months after the Games. He would also have been a favorite in the 400 meter free following his 5:28.0 in the New South Wales Championships earlier in 1908.

In the swimming events of these Games, the British entered a large, well- prepared team. Their squad produced many good performances in all six events. Unfortunately, the other strong swimming nations – Australia, Germany, Hungary, Sweden and the USA — only had token entries.

Just two years after winning a first, second and third at the Interim Games, Henry Taylor proved to be even better in his "home" Games. The little Englishman won the 400 meter and 1500 meter freestyles and anchored the winning 4 x 200 meter freestyle relay. Thanks to Taylor and his teammates, these Games were England's "finest hour" in swimming.

100 Meter Freestyle: With the exception of Cecil Healy, all of the world's fastest were present for the premier event of the 2008 Games, the 100-meter freestyle. Without Healy, the 100 free shaped up to be a fine contest between Hungary's Zoltan Halmay, the 1904 winner, and the USA's Charles Daniels, the 1906 Interim Games champion. The slender American gave away size and strength to his Hungarian rival, who stood six feet 1-1/2 inches and weighed 184 pounds (82 kg).

In the preliminaries, Daniels bettered Cecil Healy's world long course best of 1:07.4 with a brilliant 1:05.8, equaling Halmay's world record, swum in a 25-meter course in 1905. In an earlier heat, the big Hungarian had won easily in 1:08.2, well ahead of the rest of the field. The semifinals saw the two favorites slow down to save themselves for the final.

In the final, Halmay immediately sprinted to the fore, following his powerful dive, but Daniels was able to catch him at 30 meters. For the next 20 meters, the two rivals swam stroke-for-stroke, with Harald Julin of Sweden just behind them. After the midpoint of the race, Daniels began to draw ahead and it was the American who touched first in the world record time of 1:05.6. Only a meter back. Halmay finished with an excellent time of 1:06.2, Julin took the bronze in 1:08.0.

400 Meter Freestyle: Henry Taylor (GBR) and Otto Scheff (AUT) looked to be the favorites for this event with Cecil Healy (AUS) – the swimmer with the world's best time for this event in 1908 — unable to attend the Games. Taylor and Scheff were expected to stage another close, two-man race similar to their 1906 contest near Athens. However, there was a third strong contender for this Olympic title, Frank Beaurepaire, the young Australian champion, who had posted 5:28.4 — the year's fastest time.

Taylor a short 23-year-old Englishman from Hyde Seal SC, won his heat in an Olympic record 5:42.2. Teammate Sydney Battersby from Weston-Super-Mere, the 17-year old Beaurepaire from Melbourne and Scheff won their heats comfortably in 5:48.8, 5:49.2 and 5:52.2 respectively.

The real racing began in the semifinals. Scheff just touched out Taylor in the first semi by a scant 4-tenths of a second. Both swimmers broke Taylor's Olympic mark

Britain's Henry Taylor was a triple winner at the 1908 Games, setting world records in the 400 and 1500-meter freestyle events and anchoring Britain's winning freestyle relay.

with times of 5:40.6 and 5:41.0. Battersby, less than four meters behind, did not qualify for the finals. Beaurepaire captured the other semi over William Foster from Liverpool, England, in a respectable 5:44.0 without fully extending himself.

In the final, Taylor swam a controlled first 300 meters before overpowering his two teenage rivals over the last hundred. His time of 5:36.8 was a world mark since FINA did not accept Barney Kieran's 5:25.3, swum in Sydney in 1905, nor his 5:22.2 from Southport, England, in 1906. Beaurepaire, using a strong final length, beat Scheff for second, 5:44.0 to 5:46.0.

1500 Meter Freestyle: Taylor entered the Games as a slight favorite over Scheff and Beaurepaire in the 1500 meter freestyle due to his success in Athens in 1906 and the fact that he was at home. However, earlier in the year, Scheff had successfully defended his Austrian mile title in 25:44.4, while Beaurepaire had taken his first Australian mile crown in 24:49.0 in fast salt water.

This longest Olympic race proved to be a very tough struggle, as Taylor, Battersby and Beaurepaire battled for the gold. In the preliminaries, these three were well clear of the rest of the field with the only performances under 24 minutes.

Arno Bieberstein (GER)

Taylor's 23:24.4 in the sixth heat was the new Olympic best after Beaurepaire and Battersby had successively set the record at 23:45.8 and 23:42.5 in earlier heats.

In the first semifinal, Taylor swam away from Beaurepaire over the last half to drop his own Olympic and world record by half a minute to 22:54.0, with the little Australian finishing in 23:25.4. In the other semi, Battersby outswam Scheff by over a minute in 23:23.0, with John Jarvis, the English double distance champion of the 1900 Games, dropping out early in the race.

After the world record swim by Taylor in the semis, few were expecting the final to be a real contest. However, it turned out to be a three-man fight all the way, with Taylor ultimately eking out the win over the final 100 meters in the world record time of 22:48.4 .Battersby, after gaining second over his Australian rival, 22:51.2 to 22:56.2, continued for another 109-plus meters to set a world record of 24:33.0 for the mile. All of the finalists had been offered the option to be timed officially for this longer distance.

100 Meter Backstroke: Arno Bieberstein, from the famous German club Hellas Magdeburg, was the world's best backstroker from 1906 through 1909. His world long course best time of 1:21.0 at this distance was not beaten until 1912. In London, the 24-year-old German cruised through all three rounds of the 100-meter dorsal event, eventually swimming to a two-second win over Ludwig Dam of Denmark, 1:24.6 to 1:26.6. Herbert Haresnape, an Englishman from Liverpool, finished third in 1:27.0.

200 Meter Breaststroke: Before the London Games, the world best long course time was 3:04.4 by Erich Seidel of Germany in 1904. This very fast record was not approached in London and was not bettered until 1912. Fred Holman, a 25-year-old Englishman from Exeter, swept through all three rounds in these Games to give Britain yet another Olympic title. In each of his three races, he won with a strong second 100. His times, in order, were 3:10.6, 3:10.0 and 3:09.2. William Robinson, age 38 from Liverpool, outswam Pontus Hansson from Stockholm, Sweden for the silver medal, 3:12.8 to 3:14.6., becoming the oldest Olympic swimming medalist. Ironically Seidel was eliminated after the semifinals.

Britain's Fred Holman won the 200-m breaststroke ahead of 38-year-old teammate Bill Robinson.

4 x 200 Meter Freestyle Relay: Perhaps Henry Taylor's finest Olympic performance came in the 4 x 200 meter relay final. After Hungary had led for the first three legs with Britain in third, the little Englishman started more than eight seconds behind Zoltan Halmay and over three seconds behind the USA's Leslie Rich. In the second 100 meters of his anchor leg, Taylor made up two body lengths on Rich of the US and much more on the Hungarian, who seemed to collapse as Taylor went past. Taylor's split of 2:37.0 helped his country to post a world record of 10:55.6. Only 200-meter specialists Charles Daniels of the USA and Barney Kieran of Australia had swum the double century faster up to that time.

Britain's triumphant 4 x 200-m freestyle relay. From left: Radmilovic, Foster, Derbyshire, and Taylor with Coach W. Brickett.

The Birth of FINA: After having allowed host nations to organize Olympic and other international swimming events according to their own rules for more than a dozen years, it had become abundantly clear that there was an urgent need to standardize the rules and events of the sport. An international organization was needed to form and administer the rules of competition.

George Hearn (GBR), president of the English Amateur Swimming Association, planned and held just such a meeting at the Manchester Hotel in London on July 19, 1908 during the London Games. Assisting him in this task of forming a swimming federation were Bill Henry (GBR), the pool designer; Max Ritter, a 22-year-old German swimmer; and Hjalmar Johansson (SWE), the high diving winner of the 1908 Games. A Formative Congress was held, attended by delegates from England, Belgium, Denmark, Finland, France, Germany, Hungary, Ireland, Sweden and Wales. The result was the creation of FINA, following the model of the English ASA.

The purpose of FINA was: 1) to establish and control swimming, diving and water polo rules for all amateur competition; 2) to establish the events and control the conditions for all world records; and 3) to organize and administer Olympic swimming, diving and water polo competitions.

1 9 0 8   O L Y M P I C   S W I M M I N G   R E S U L T S
L O N D O N ,   E N G L A N D - 1 0 0   M E T E R   O U T D O O R   P O O L

Men's 100 Meter Freestyle:		Trial		Semi		Final	
1) Charles Daniels	USA	Wo1:05.8	V	1:10.2	II	Wo1:05.6	
2) Zoltan Halmay	HUN	01:08.2	I	1:09.4	I	1:06.2	
3) Harald Julin	SWE	1:12.0	IV	1:10.2	I	1:08.0	
4 Leslie Rich	USA	1:14.6	IX	1:10.8	II	No Time	
Harry Hebner	USA	1:11.0	VI	1:11.8	I		
GS Dockrell	GBR	1:13.2	VIII	1:14.0	II		
Otto Scheff	AUT	1:11.4	II	No Time	II		
Frank Beaurepaire	AUS	1:13.2	V	No Time	I		
Paul Radmilovic	GBR	1:12.0	VI	No Time	I		
A. Tyldlesley	GBR	1:12.0	II	No Time	II		
Rob Derbyshire	GBR	1:12.6	IV				
Jozsef Onody	HUN	1:13.2	V				
L. Benenga	NED	1:14.0	III				
C.W. Edwards	GBR	1:15.8	VII	No Time	I		
A. Deprez	BEL	1:16.0	IX				
R. Zimmerman	CAN	1:35.0	VII				
Theadore Tartakover	AUS	No Time	I				
B. Benenga	NED	No Time	I				
H. Meyboon	BEL	No Time	I				
HRS Klem	DEN	No Time	I				
D. Baivado	ITA	No Time	I				
Gerard Meister	FRA	No Time	II				
Jozsef Munk	HUN	No Time	II				
CD Trubenbach	USA	No Time	II				
Hj SaxdorPoul Holm	DEN	No Time	III				
Henrik Hajos	HUN	No Time	III				
Robert Andersson	SWE	No Time	III				
RB Foster	USA	No Time	IV				
V. Boin	BEL	No Time	IV				
G, Innocent	GBR	No Time					
R. Andre	FRA	No Time	V				
Hj. Saxtorph	DEN	No Time	V				
F. Feyaerts	BEL	No Time	VI				
EJL Cooke	AUS	No Time	VI				

Men's 400 Meter Freestyle:		Trial		Semi		Final	
1) Henry Taylor	GBR	Lo5:42.2	VI	5:41.0	I	Wo5:36.8	
2) Frank Beaurepaire	AUS	5:49.2	IV	5:44.0	II	5:44.2	
3) Otto Scheff	AUT	5:52.2	VII	Lo5:40.6	I	5:46.0	
4 William Foster	GBR	5:54.8	II	5:52.2	II	No Time	
Sydney Battersby	GBR	o5:48.8	I	No Time	I		
Bela Lastorres	HUN	5:52.2	I	No Time	I		
Paul Radmilovic	GBR	6:10.0	V	No Time	II		
Imre Zacher	HUN	6:09.8	VIII	DNF	II		
Fred Springfield	AUS	5:57.4	VI				
Sam Blatherwick	GBR	6:16.8	IV				

Name	Country	Time	
H. Hajos	HUN	6:19.8	IX
WH Haynes	GBR	6:21.2	VII
Robert Andersson	SWE	6:28.0	II
Theadore Tartakover	AUS	6:35.0	III
AT Sharp	GBR	7:00.8	IX
Leo "Bud" Goodwin	USA	No Time	I
Vilhelm Andersson	SWE	No Time	I
CD Trubebbach	USA	No Time	IV
D. Baiardo	ITA	No Time	IV
Poul Holm	DEN	No Time	V
Mario Massa	ITA	No Time	VI
Jozsef Onody	HUN	No Time	VII
FW Meiuning	NED	No Time	VII
Hj. Saxdorph	DEN	No Time	VII
H. Decoin	FRA	DNF	

Men's 1500 Meter Freestyle:

Name	Country	Trial		Semi		Final
1) Henry Taylor	GBR	o23:24.4	VI	Lo22:54.0	I	Wo22:48.4
2) Sydney Battersby	GBR	o23:42.5	IV	o23:23.0	II	22:51.2
3) Frank Beaurepaire	AUS	o23:45.8	II	23:25.4	I	22:56.2
Otto Scheff	AUT	24:15.8	VI	24:25.4	II	DNS
William Foster	GBR	24:33.4	VII	No Time	I	
L. Moist	GBR	26:52.0	III	No Time	I	
Fred Springfield	AUS	24:52.4	IV			
Paul Radmilovic	GBR	25:02.4	I	DNS II		
S. Blatherwick	GBR	25:05.4	II			
John Jarvis	GBR	25:51.6	V	DNF II		
Gunnar Wennerstorm	SWE	27:15.4	I			
PL Ooms	NED	27:24.4	II			
Vilhelm Anderson	SWE	27:34.4	II			
JB Green	USA	28:09.0	V			
RH Hassell	GBR	28:14.8	V			
G. Wretman	SWE	28:40.8	VI			
O. Muzzi	ITA	28:52.6	I			
AA Theuriet	FRA	32:37.0	IV			
E. Meyer	NED	No Time	VI			

Men's 100 Meter Backstroke:

Name	Country	Trial		Semi		Final
1) Arno Bieberstein	GER	o1:25.6	I	o1:25.6	I	o1:24.6
2) Ludvig Dam	DEN	1:26.4	IV	No Time	I	1:26.6
3) Herbert Haresnape	GBR	1:26.2	IV	1:28.8	II	1:27.0
4 Gustav Aurick	GER	1:27.4	VI	1:28.2	II	No Time
JR Taylor	GBR	1:25.8	VI	No Time	II	
Max Ritter	GER	1:33.4	II	No Time	I	
S. Parvin	GBR	1:30.2	V	No Time	I	
P. Lewis	GBR	1:31.0	III	No Time	II	
AM Goessling	USA	1:29.0	VI			
S. Willis	GBR	1:34.4	II			
BA Roadenburch	NED	1:36.2	III			
H. Jonsson	FIN	No Time	I			

J. Hendricksson	FIN	No Time II						
R. Zimmerman	CAN	No Time III						
A. Beretta	ITA	No Time IV						
Gustaf Wretman	SWE	No Time VI						
O. Gregoire II	BEL	DNF VI						
G. Corlever	NED	No Time VII						
E. Seaward	GBR	DQ VII						
Sandor Kugler	HUN	DQ VII						

Men's 200 Meter Breaststroke:		Trial		Semi		Final
1) Fred Holman	GBR	o3:10.6	I	o3:10.0	I	o3:09.2
2) William Robinson	GBR	3:13.0	V	3:11.8	II	3:12.8
3) Pontus Hansson	SWE	3:15.0	IV	3:13.0	II	3:14.6
4 Odin Toldy	HUN	3:14.4	IV	3:16.4	I	3:15.2
Erich Seidel	GER	3:17.2	III	No Time	I	
WA Persson	SWE	3:16.4	II	No Time	II	
Jozsef Fabinyi	HUN	3:17.6	VI	No Time	I	
Felicien Courbet	BEL	3:16.4	VII	No Time	I	
Andras Baronyi	HUN	3:18.0	II			
R. Rosler	GER	3:18.0	I			
Percy Courtman	GBR	3:19.4	VII			
KT Kumfeldt	SWE	3:24.6	VI			
PO Fjastad	SWE	3:31.4	V			
M. Gumpel	SWE	No Time	I			
AM Goersling	USA	No Time	II			
Herman Cederberg	FIN	No Time	II			
FH Naylor	GBR	No Time	II			
H. Johanssen	SWE	No Time	III (5 Yds back)			
A. Davies	GBR	No Time	III			
P. Strauwen	BEL	No Time	III			
SH Gooday	GBR	No Time	IV			
A. Beretta	ITA	No Time	IV			
JH Henrikssen	FIN	No Time	V			
EJL Cooke	AUS	No Time	V			
H. Klem	DEN	No Time	VI			
HJ Jonsson	FIN	No Time	VI			
CA Andersson	SWE	o Time	VII			

Men's 4x200 Meter Freestyle Relay:	Trial		Final
1) GBR (Derbyshire,Radmilovic,Foster,Taylor)	Lo10:53.6	II	10:55.6
2) HUN (Munk,Zachar,Lastorres,Halmay)	No Time	III	10:59.0
3) USA (Hebner,Goodwin,Daniels,Rich)	11:01.4	II	11:02.8
4 xAUS (Beaurepaire,Springfield,Baker,Tartakover)	11:35.0	I	No Time
DEN	12:53.0	I	

W World Record, L World LC Best, o Olympic Record, x Australasia

1908 Men's Olympic Swimming Medals

	Gold	Medals
GBR	4	7
USA	1	2
GER	1	1
AUS	0	2
HUN	0	2
SWE	0	2
AUT	0	1
DEN	0	1

1896–1908 Men's Olympic Swimming Medals

	Gold	Medals
GER	7	11
GBR	6	10
HUN	4	11
USA	3	13
AUS	2	4
AUT	1	8
FRA	1	4
GRE	0	5
NED	0	1
SWE	0	2
DEN	0	2

1 9 1 2: Stockholm, Sweden
(100 Meter Outdoor Course)

The 100-meter Olympic racing course in Stockholm (1912)

The International Swimming Federation (FINA) ran the swimming, diving and water polo events in Stockholm in 1912. For the first time ever, the events and rules of competition were standardized on an international basis. This was a giant step forward for the sport of swimming at the Olympic level.

For the aquatic contests, a 100 meter course was constructed in the cold water of Djurgardsbrunnsviken, a waterway open to the sea just outside of Stockholm. Much wider (six lanes) than the London pool, this course was free of currents.

Full teams were sent to Sweden from all of the leading swimming countries: Great Britain, USA, Australasia (Australia and New Zealand), Hungary, Germany, Austria and Sweden. Strong delegations also arrived from many other nations. However, most of these fine competitors were little known swimmers at their first Olympic Games. Frank Beaurepaire (AUS) and Charlie Daniels (USA) were the most notable missing champions. The former was kept at home by his federation for working in physical education, while the latter retired after the 1911 Indoor NAAU Championships.

Men's 100 Meter Freestyle: One of the most impressive of the new generation of Olympic swimming stars in Stockholm was Duke Kahanamoku (USA) from the Hui Nalu Club in Honolulu, Hawaii. This tall twenty-two year old was of royal Hawaiian descent and a product of surfing on the mighty waves off Oahu.

Twenty year-old Duke Kahanamoku, of royal Hawaiian descent, set a world record of 1:02.6 in the semifinals of the 100-meter freestyle, then breezed to victory in the final.

He was unheard of until 1911 when he set American long course records in the 50 and 100 yard freestyle. His 100 yard record of 55.4, equal to 1:02+ for 100 meters, was about a second faster than Cecil Healy's world best long course 100 meter time of 1:03.2 from 1908. Healy; William Longworth, the Australian champion of 1912; and Kurt Bretting, the top German sprinter, from the Hellas Magdeburg Club, were the other leading medal possibilities in this event.

In the fifth heat of the Stockholm 100 meter contest, the "Duke" lowered the world record to 1:02.6. Earlier, fellow American Perry McGillivray from Chicago had dropped Daniels' 1908 Olympic mark from 1:05.6 to 1:04.8. Kahanamoku led the field through the quarter-finals with a modest 1:03.8, slightly faster than Ken Huszagh (USA) and Bretting. These last two swimmers both won their second round races in 1:04.2.

Through a misunderstanding, the three American entries were not present for the start of the semifinals. However, upon the request of Healy, the meet committee permitted the USA swimmers to start in an extra heat. This allowed Kahanamoku (1:02.4) and Huszagh (1:06.2) to qualify for the final. The Duke's time bettered his earlier world and Olympic standards.

In the final, the tall Hawaiian eased off in the back half of the race to win in 1:03.4, as Healy sprinted home to capture second in 1:04.6, well in front of Huszagh. Bretting just missed a medal with his 1:05.8 Ten days later, the newly-crowned Olympic champion attended the German National Championships in Hamburg, where he streaked to a stunning 1:01.6 over a salt-water straightaway, a world record.

Men's 400 Meter Freestyle: Based upon pre-Games performances, the three strongest medal prospects were all Australians: Frank Beaurepaire, the 1908 silver medalist; William Longworth, who had won the New South Wales title half a year before the Games in 5:26.4; and Harold Hardwick, the Australian champion of 1911 with a 5:35.0. The outsiders were Bela Lastorres of Hungary and the little-known George Hodgson from the Montreal AA in Canada, who had swum well at the 1911 Empire Mile in London. Unfortunately, Beaurepaire missed these Games, and Longworth became sick in Stockholm at the start of the swimming races.

In the heats, Cecil Healy, Hardwick and Lastorres all dipped under Henry Taylor's 1908 Olympic record of 5:36.8 with times of 5:34.0, 5:36.0 and 5:36.3, respectively. In the first semifinal, Hodgson fought off fast-finishing Jack Hatfield from England's Middlesboro Swim Club, 5:25.5 to 5:25.6, to lower the Olympic mark for this event. Hardwick finished well ahead of Lastorres and Healy to take the second semi in 5:31.0 to 5:34.8 for the Hungarian and 5:37.8 for his fellow Australian. Malcolm Champion, Australasia's New Zealander, and Taylor, the British winner of this event in 1908, did not qualify for the final, as they finished in 5:38.0 and 5:48.2.

In what later became a three-man race, Hodgson and Hardwick passed through the first half of the final together with Hatfield close behind. Over the third 100, the little Englishman caught Hardwick as Hodgson took the lead, then pulled away from his Australian rival at the start of the final length. However, Hatfield could not catch the Canadian, who won by two meters

Canada celebrated its first Olympic gold medalist in 1912, when George Hodgson, from Montreal, upset the favored Australians to take the 400- and 1500-meter freestyle, setting a world record of 22:00.0 in the "metric mile."

with a record time of 5:24.4 to 5:25.8. Hardwick easily beat Healy for third, 5:31.2 to 5:37.8.

Men's 1500 Meter Freestyle: William Longworth (AUS) was the clear pre- race favorite for this longest of all Olympic events because of his dominant performances in Australia. The year before Stockholm, he swam 14 seconds under the Olympic record from 1908. Tragically his illness at the Games kept him from performing even close to his potential. In his place, George Hodgson (CAN) and the new English champion, Jack Hatfield, battled for top honors.

In the third heat, Hodgson broke Henry Taylor's world and Olympic record from 1908 by more than 25 seconds, finishing in 22:23.0 — more than 40 seconds ahead of second-place Longworth.

The first semi saw Hatfield come within several body lengths of the Canadian with a strong final 10 meters, losing 22:33.4 to the Canadian's 22:26.0. Harold Hardwick of Australia was a remote third. In the other semifinal, Hungarian Bela Lastorres won easily over Malcolm Champion from New Zealand and Great Britain's

William Foster, 23:09.8 to 23:24.2 and 23:32.1.

Hodgson quickly showed he was the class of the field in the final by sprinting to a 10-meter lead in the first 100. Steadily pulling away, he set three world marks in the event: 14:37.0 for 1000 meters, 22:00.0 at the finish of the 1500 and 23:34.5 for the mile. Hatfield, a remote second in 22:39.0, was far ahead of third-place Hardwick, 23:15.4. Champion and Lastorres dropped out before the finish.

The USA's Harry Hebner revolutionized the backstroke at the Stockholm Games. Using a rapid, alternating arm stroke and a strong flutter kick, he crushed the field in the 100-meter backstroke, setting a world record of 1:20.8.

Men's 100 Meter Backstroke: As Arno Bieberstein of Germany had dominated the 1908 Olympic backstroke so did Harry Hebner (USA) at Stockholm. With his rapid alternating arm stroke and strong flutter kick, the dorsal king from Chicago raced through all three rounds of the event without any strong opposition. In the semifinal, he beat Bieberstein's world long course best of 1:21.0 from 1906 with a 1:20.8. A false start in the final prevented a further lowering of the time. Still, Hebner won in a respectable 1:21.1 with Germans Otto Fahr (SV Cannstatt) and Paul Kellner (Berlin) second and third in 1:22.4 and 1:24.0, respectively.

Men's 200 Meter Breaststroke: The breaststroke king of the Stockholm Games was Walther Bathe of the ASV Breslau Club in Germany. Only 19, he won both the 200 and 400 meter events in this stroke. In the shorter contest, he set Olympic and world long course best times in all three rounds with times of 3:03.4, 3:02.2 and 3:01.8. Behind him in the final were two other Germans: Wilhelm Lutzow from Hellas Magdeburg, and Kurt Malisch, Bathe's club teammate from ASV Breslau, with final times of 3:05.0 and 3:08.0, respectively. Only Englishman Percy Courtman of Old Trafford SC was close to this victorious trio with a fourth place 3:08.8 in the final.

Men's 400 Meter Breaststroke: Germany's Walther Bathe controlled this event, except for the semifinal round, in which he was just able to out-touch Thor Henning (SWE) of Neptun Stockholm at the finish, with both men timed in 6:32.0. In the final, Bathe led the entire race, passing through the halfway mark in 3:03 before going on to win by six seconds in Olympic record time of 6:29.6. Henning took second (6:35.6) after a fierce struggle with Percy Courtman (GBR) and Kurt Malisch (GER) who finished in 6:36.6 and 6:37.0.

Nineteen year-old German, Walther Bathe, was king of the breast-stroke at the Stockholm Games, winning both the 200 and 400-meter events, the shorter race in a world record 3:01.8.

Men's 4 x 200 Meter Freestyle Relay: Australia and New Zealand combined as "Australasia," and were able to capture the relay final easily in 10:11.6, a world record and more than ten seconds per man faster than Britain's winning performance of 1908. The main reason for this huge drop in time was probably due to the change from trudgen to the faster crawl stroke. Had William Longworth been in good health at these Games, Australia, by itself, could have swum even faster since the only New Zealander on the winning relay was Malcolm Champion. Earlier in the year, Longworth had swum 200 meters in 2:27 — six seconds faster than the time of the average Australasian leg
in Stockholm.

After Australasia and the USA had each won its respective heat comfortably in Olympic record time, there was anticipation of a close final between these two fine teams. At first, it looked as though that would be the case as Australia's Cecil Healy and the USA's Ken Huszagh swam their leadoff legs in tandem, touching the wall simultaneously. But Champion opened up a 10-meter lead over Harry Hebner on the second leg. Leslie Boardman then extended the lead another five meters over Perry McGillivray. On the anchor leg, Harold Hardwick held Duke Kahanamoku at bay, as the valiant Hawaiian was unable to close the gap on the determined Aussie. At the finish it was Australasia by 15 meters in a world record 10:11.6. The USA (10:20.2) finished eight seconds ahead of Britain (10:28.2), which was nearly nine seconds in front of fourth-place Germany.

An "Australasian" squad consisting of three Aussies and a New Zealander combined to win the 4x200-meter freestyle relay. From left: Champion, Hardwick, Healy, and Boardman.

1912 WOMEN'S EVENTS

After much debate, the IOC decided to add swimming competition for women to the Olympic Games. Two events were selected: the 100 meter freestyle and the 4x100 meter freestyle relay. Support for this addition to the Olympic program came primarily from Australia, Great Britain and much of western Europe. With 25 entries and fast times, including a world record, women's swimming made a successful debut in the Olympic Games. This did much to encourage other European countries as well as the United States to start holding women's national championships and to enter the women's events at the next Olympic Games.

Fanny Durack and Mina Wylie gave Australia a one-two sweep in the first-ever Olympic event for women, the 100-meter freestyle at the 1912 Games, with Durack setting a world record (1:19.8). It would be 44 years before the Aussie women would win another gold medal in swimming.

Women's 100 Meter Freestyle: Fanny Durack, a 22 year–old Australian, was the class of the women's 100 meter freestyle field. In the preliminaries, she bettered the world record held by England's Daisy Curwen, by 8-tenths of a second with a 1:19.8 before winning her semifinal in 1:20.2 and the final in 1:22.2. No other swimmer even came close to any of Durack's times as Wilhelmina Wylie, also from Sydney, finished second in 1:25.4, well ahead of Englishwoman Jennie Fletcher (1:27.0). Unfortunately, Curwen, the former world record-holder, was whisked to the hospital for an operation after swimming 1:23.6 in her heat and posting the second-fastest time in the semis. Sadly, she was unable to battle Durack for the gold in the final.

Women's 4 x 100 Meter Freestyle Relay: Only four teams entered the relay competition. In fact, Australasia was unable to find the funds to take two more women to Stockholm and thus did not even field a relay team. Even without Daisy Curwen, Great Britain proved to have the most depth as Bella Moore, Jennie Fletcher, Annie Speirs and Irene Steer clocked 5:52.8 for the win, nearly 12 seconds ahead of runner-up Germany (6:04.6). Austria was third at 6:17.0.

Great Britain's winning women's 4 x 100-meter freestyle relay, with the team's official chaperone in the center. From Left: Moore, Fletcher, Chaperone Miss ?, Speirs and Steer.

Men's 100 Meter Freestyle:		Trial		2nd Round		Semi		Final
1) Duke Kahanamoku	USA	Lo1:02.6	V	1:03.8	II	Lo1:02.4	III	1:03.4
2) Cecil Healy	AUS	1:05.2	IV	1:04.8	III	1:05.6	I	1:04.6
3) Ken Huszagh	USA	1:06.2	IV	1:04.2	III	1:06.2	III	1:05.6
4 Kurt Bretting	GER	1:07.0	II	1:04.2	I	1:04.6	II	1:05.8
5 Walter Ramme	GER	1:10.2	VII	1:07.8	II	1:05.8	I	1:06.4
William Longworth	AUS	1:05.2	V	1:05.2	I	1:06.2	I	DNS
Perry McGillivray	USA	o1:04.8	IV	1:04.4	III	1:06.2	III	
Leslie Boardman	AUS	1:06.0	III	1:05.4	III			
Harold Hardwick	AUS	1:05.8	VI	1:06.0	I			
Nick Nerich	USA	1:07.6	III	1:08.8	II			
Max Ritter	GER	1:08.0	VI	1:08.8	II			
Robert Andersson	SWE	1:09.2	I	1:19.0	III			
Ladislav Belesney	HUN	1:08.0	I					
Rob Derbyshire	GBR	1:09.2	III					
Harry Hebner	USA	1:10.4	V					
Harald Julin	SWE	1:11.8	VII					
Mario Massa	ITA	1:11.8	VII					
Theador Tartakover	AUS	1:12.2	II					
Eris Berquist	SWE	1:13.4	VIII					
Jules Wuyts	BEL	1:13.6	II					
Andre AssimaCopuolo	GRE	1:15.4	I					
Herman Meyboom	BEL	1:15.4	VI					
Gerard Meister	FRA	1:26.6	V					
Georges Rigal	FRA	1:17.8	VIII					
John H Johnsen	NOR	1:19.1	VII					
Herbert von Kuhlberg	RUS	No Time I						
David Baiardo	ITA	No Time III						
Walther Binner	GER	No Time III						
Akois Kenyery	HUN	No Time III						
Eric Andersson	SWE	No Time IV						
Georg Kunisch	GER	No Time IV						
Jim Reilly	USA	No Time VI						
Ladislaus Szentgrothy	HUN	No Time VIII						

Men's 400 Meter Freestyle:		Trial		Semi		Final
1) William Hodgson	CAN	5:50.6	VI	o5:25.4	I	o5:24.4
2) Jack Hatfield	GBR	5:35.6	V	5:25.6	I	5:25.8
3) Harold Hardwick	AUS	o5:36.0	I	5:31.0	II	5:31.2
4 Cecil Healy	AUS	o5:34.0	V	5:37.8	II	5:37.8
5 Bela Lastorres	HUN	5:36.3	IV	5:34.8	II	5:42.0
Malcolm Champion	AUS(NZL)	5:37.0	I	5:38.0	II	
Henry Taylor	GBR	5:48.4	IV	5:48.2	II	
William Foster	GBR	5:52.4	VI	5:49.0	I	

Nick Nerich	USA	5:50.4	II	5:51.0	I	
Sidney Battersby	GBR	6:03.6	II	5:51.2	I	
John H Johnsen	NOR	6:14.4	II	No Time	I	
Max Ritter	GER	5:44.6	III			
Alois Kenyery	HUN	5:46.0	III			
Oscar Schiele	GER	5:57.0	VI			
Franz Schuh	AUT	6:09.6	V			
Jim Reilly	USA	6:10.2	I			
Nils Erik Haglund	SWE	6:23.4	I			
Johan Wedholm	SWE	6:29.8	II			
George Godfrey	SAF	6:30.6	VI			
Harry Hedegaard	DEN	7:07.8	VI			
David Baiardo	ITA	No Time	I			
Mario Massa	ITA	DNF	I			
Parell Awksentjeff	RUS	DNF	II			
BD Teander	SWE	DNF	III			
Theadore Tartakover	AUS	DNF	III			
Nicolas Woronkoff	RUS	DNF	IV			

Men's 1500 Meter Freestyle:		Trial		Semi		Final	
1) George Hodgson	CAN	Lo22:23.0	III	22:26.0	I	Wo22:00.0	
2) Jack Hatfield	GBR	23:16.6	II	22:33.4	I	22:39.0	
3) Harold Hardwick	AUS	23:23.2	V	23:14.0	I	23:15.4	
Malcolm Champion	NZL	23:34.0	I	23:24.2	II	DNF	
Bela Lastorres	HUN	22:58.0	II	23:09.8	II	DNF	
Vilhelm Anderson	SWE	23:12.2	I	23:14.2	I		
William Foster	GBR	23:52.2	V	23:32.1	II		
William Longworth	AUS	23:03.6	III	DNS	II		
Sydney Battersby	GBR	23:58.0	IV	DNS	II		
Henry Taylor	GBR	24:06.4	I	DNF	I		
Franz Schuh	AUT	25:19.8	IV	DNS	I		
John H Johnsen	DEN	25:45.6	V				
Karl Gustav Collin	SWE	27:05.2	V				
Johan Wedholm	SWE	27:38.0	IV				
Harry Hedegaard	DEN	28:32.4	III				
Herbert Wetter	NOR	DNF	I				
Auguste Caby	FRA	DNF	II				
Mario Massa	ITA	DNF	IV				
Parell Awksentjeff	RUS	DNF	V				

Men's 100 Meter Backstroke:		Trial		Semi		Final	
1) Harry Hebner	USA	Lo1:21.0	I	Lo1:20.8	I	1:21.2	
2) Otto Fahr	GER	1:22.4	II	1:21.8	I	1:22.4	
3) Paul Kellner	GER	1:26.0	II	1:26.2	I	1:24.0	
4 Andras Baronyi	HUN	1:22.0	III	1:26.2	I	1:25.2	
5 Otto Gross	GER	1:24.0	I	1:26.0	II	1:25.8	
Ladislaus Szentgrothy	HUN	1:26.6	V	1:26.4	I		
Herbert Haresknape	GBR	1:27.0I	V	1:26.8	II		

Frank Sandon	GBR	1:31.8	V	1:32.2	II		
Eric Schultze	GER	1:27.2	IV	No Time	I		
George Webster	GBR	1:29.4	II	No Time	I		
O. Gregoire	BEL	1:29.8	II				
Gunnar Sundman	SWE	1:31.2	IV	1:35.0	II		
Ake Bergnan	SWE	1:33.8	I				
John H Johnsen	NOR	1:34.2	V				
K. Lundevall	SWE	1:46.8	II				
Harry Svendsen	NOR	1:47.2	III				
Oscar Schiele	GER	DQ	I				
Johann Wenk	HUN	DQ1:28.6	II				

Men's 200 Meter Breaststroke:

		Trial		Semi		Final	
1) Walter Bathe	GER	Lo3:03.4	IV	Lo3:02.2	II	Lo3:01.8	
2) Wilhelm Lutzow	GER	o3:07.4	I	3:04.4	II	3:05.0	
3) Paul Malisch	GER	3:08.8	II	3:09.6	I	3:08.0	
4 Percy Courtman	GBR	3:09.8	IV	3:09.4	II	3:08.8	
Thor Henning	SWE	3:14.0	I	3:10.4	I	DNF	
Harald Julin	SWE	3:12.8	VI	3:10.6	I		
Oscar Demjan	HUN	3:07.8	VI	3:11.2	II		
Felicien Courbet	BEL	3:12.4	V	3:11.6	II		
Karl Gustaf Lindroos	FIN	3:16.4	I	3:11.6	I		
Carlyle Atkinson	GBR	3:12.0	III	3:15.2	I		
Arvo O Aaltonen	FIN	3:13.0	II	3:17.0	I		
Pontus Hansson	SWE	3:14.2	V	DNS	II		
George Innocent	GBR	3:16.0	V				
Herman Cederberg	FIN	3:18.6	VI				
Nils Gustav Andersson	SWE	3:20.6	II				
Wilhelm Lindgren	FIN	3:21.2	VI				
Fredrik Lowenadler	SWE	3:22.2	IV				
Frank Schryver	AUS	3:24.0	I				
Sven Hansson	SWE	3:24.4	VI				
Josef Wastl	AUT	3:25.6	II				
George Bajmakoff	RUS	3:29.0	II				
Oscar Hamren	SWE	No Time	VI				
Michael McDermott	USA	DQ3:18.2	IV				
Auden Rusten	NOR	DQ3:39.8	V				

Men's 400 Meter Breaststroke:

		Trial		Semi		Final	
1) Walter Bathe	GER	Lo6:34.6	V	Lo6:32.0	I	Lo6:29.6	
2) Thor Henning	SWE	o6:52.4	I	o6:32.0	I	6:35.6	
3) Percy Courtman	GBR	o6:43.8	IV	6:36.6	I	6:36.4	
4 Paul Malisch	GER	o6:47.0	II	6:47.6	I	6:37.0	
Wilhelm Lutzow	GER	6:49.8	III	6:44.6	I	DNF	
Arvo O Aaltonen	FIN	6:48.8	IV	6:56.8	II		
Felicien Courbet	BEL	6:52.6	III	6:59.8	I		
Karl Gustaf Lindroos	FIN	7:00.0	II	7:00.4	II		
Zeno van Siengalewicz	AUT	7:04.0	III	DNS	I		

George Innocent	GBR	7:07.8	I	DNS	II
Frank Schryver	AUS	7:07.8	III		
Wilhelm Lindgren	FIN	7:12.6	IV		
Nils Gustav Andersson	SWE	7:17.0	II		
George Bajmakoff	RUS	7:28.6	V	DNS	I
Oscar Demjan	HUN	DQ6:35.8	I		
Mike McDermott	USA	DQ7:07.0	II		
Joseph Wastl	AUS	DNF	I		

Men's 4x200 Meter Freestyle Relay:

2:31.5 2:33.5 2:35.1 2:31.2

	Trial		Final
1) xrAUS (Healy,Champion(NZL),Boardman,Hardwick)	Lo10:14.0 II		Lo10:11.6
2) rUSA (Huszagh,Hebner,McGillivray,Kahanamoku)	Lo10:26.4 I		10:20.2
3) GBR (Foster,Battersby,Hatfield,Taylor)	10:39.4	I	10:28.2
4 rGER (Schiele,Ritter,Kunisch,Bretting)	10:42.2	II	10:37.0
HUN (Belesnay,Zachar,Kenyery,Lastorres)	10:34.6	I	DNS

r AUS,USA,GER swam different order of same entrants in heats

x Australasia

1912 Men's Olympic Swimming Medals

	Gold	Medals
GER	2	6
USA	2	4
CAN	2	2
AUS	1	4
GBR	0	4
SWE	0	1

1896 – 1912 Men's Olympic Swimming Medals

	Gold	Medals
GER	8	17
USA	5	17
GBR	6	14
HUN	4	11
AUS	3	8
CAN	2	2
AUT	1	8
FRA	1	4
GRE	0	5
SWE	0	3
DEN	0	2
NED	0	1

Women's 100 Meter Freestyle:

		Trial		Semi		Final
1) Fanny Durack	AUS	Wo1:19.8 IV		1:20.2	I	1:22.2
2) Wilhelmina Wylie	AUS	1:26.8	II	1:27.0	II	1:25.4
3) Jennie Fletcher	GBR	1:26.2	II	1:27.2	II	1:27.0
4 Grete Rosenberg	GER	1:25.0	V	1:29.2	II	1:27.2
5 Annie Spiers	GBR	1:25.6	V	1:27.0	I	1:27.4
Daisey Curwen	GBR	o1:23.6	II	1:26.8	I	DNS
Bella Moore	GBR	o1:29.8		1:27.4	I	
Mary Langford	GBR	1:28.0	III	1:29.1	I	
Louise Otto	GER	1:34.4	I	1:32.0	I	
Wally Dressel	GER	1:28.6	IV	1:33.4	II	
Irene Steer	GBR	1:27.2	IV	DQ1:29.0	II	
Hermine Stint	GER	1:29.2	III			

Josephine Sticker	AUT	1:31.8	III
Margaretr Adler	AUT	1:34.4	IV
Klara Milch	AUT	1:37.2	I
Bertha Zahhorrek	AUT	1:38.6	II
Tyyne Maria Jarvi	FIN	1:41.4	I
Peri Kellner	AUT	1:41.2	II
Greta Johansson	SWE	1:41.4	I
Vera Thulin	SWE	1:44.0	V
Karen Lundgren	SWE	1:44.8	II
Mme. Guttenstein	BEL	No Time	III
Elsa Bjorklund	SWE	No Time	III
Greta Carlssson	SWE	No Time	IV
Regina Kari	FIN	No Time	IV

4x100 Meter Freestyle Relay: Final
1) GBR (Moore,Fletcher,Speirs,Steer)   Lo5:52.8
2) GER (Dressel,Otto,Stindt,Rosenberg)   6:04.6
3) AUT   (Adler,Milch,Sticker,Zahouch)   6:17.0
4 SWE (GI Carlsson,ATM Johansson,S.Jonsson,Thulin)   No Time

W World Record, L World LC Best, o Olympic Record

1912 Women's Olympic Swimming Medals
	Gold	Medals
AUS	1	2
GBR	1	2
GER	0	1
AUT	0	1

1 9 1 6: Berlin, Germany

Unfortunately, the Olympic Games that had been awarded to Berlin, Germany for 1916 never took place due to the First World War (1914-1918). One can only speculate as to what might have happened had the Games been held. Following the 1912 Stockholm Olympics, there was great progress around the world in 1913 and 1914 among both men and women.

1920: Antwerp, Belgium
(100 Meter Fresh, Cold Water Pool)

The 100-meter Olympic Pool at the 1920 Antwerp Olympic Games.

In the euphoria of the post-war world, nearly all of the best athletes came together in Belgium for the VII Olympic Games. The exceptions were the competitors from the Central Powers: Germany, Austria and Hungary, who were banned from competing in these Games in the aftermath of the Great War. With the large number of young men killed or severely wounded and with the disruption of the political and social structures in these countries, only a few might have performed at the Olympic level. It is possible that Erich Rademacher of Hellas Magdeburg, Germany might have won one or both of the breaststroke events and that Bernhard Skamper, also from Germany, might have won a medal in backstroke. Anything more than this would have been unlikely.

The pool in Antwerp was 100 meters long, similar to the cold-water course in Stockholm. It was a fresh-water facility located near the ancient fortifications of the city. As in Sweden, the dark, cold water and low air temperature had a negative effect on the level of performance. These conditions were hardest on the entrants from lands with warm climates such as Australia and Hawaii.

With the end of the war two years earlier, some new swimmers, mostly from unscarred countries, arrived on the Olympic scene. On the men's side were Americans Warren and Pua Kealoha, William Harris, Ray Kegeris and Fred Kahele, plus Georges Vernot of Canada, Gerard Blitz from Belgium and Sweden's Hakon Malmroth. Almost unnoticed was the inaugural appearance of Japan with two swimmers in the men's events. Their high expectations were dashed when neither swimmer was able to reach a final in any of his events.

In the women's contests, all of the competitors were virtually unknown outside of their own countries, but that didn't stop them from swimming fast.

Headed by Norman Ross of the Illinois AC and Ethelda Bleibtrey from the Women's Swimming Association of New York, the USA dominated the eight men's and three women's swimming contests in Antwerp. The American totals were five firsts and 11 medals for the men plus all three of the firsts and seven medals for the women.

1920 MEN'S EVENTS

After a collision, the final of the 100-meter free had to be re-swum, but the result was the same: Duke Kahanamoku defended his Olympic crown as he led a one-two-three Hawaiian sweep.

Men's 100 Meter Freestyle: Thirty year-old Duke Kahanamoku, the 1912 Games winner and world record-holder in this event was the clear favorite for the 1920 Olympic title. Behind him, with the best chances for the medals were three other Americans: Norman Ross (Illinois AC), the multi-event winner from the 1919 Inter Allied Games in Paris; Pua Kealoha (Hui Makani Club); and William Harris (Outrigger Canoe Club). Curiously, three of these four came from different Honolulu clubs. Kealoha and Harris were second and third behind the Duke at the American Tryouts in Chicago, held a month before the Games. No one from any other country appeared to be a serious contender.

Once again, Kahanamoku became the Olympic sprint king. He led his American teammates, through the trials, semis, final and reswim of the final with times of 1:01.8, 1:01.4, 1:00.4 and 1:01.4, respectively. All of his times were well below his 1912 Olympic mark of 1:02.4, with his final performance one second better than his world record from 1918. Unfortunately, a reswim was necessitated by a collision between William Herald of Australia and Ross in the final. However, the order of finish remained the same with Kahanamoku (1:01.4), Kealoha (1:02.2) and Harris (1:03.0) earning the medals. Ross elected not to enter the reswim even though he had come in fourth in the final.

Men's 400 Meter Freestyle:

Slender Ludy Langer (USA) from the Los Angeles AC was the leading 400 meter freestyler in the world from 1914 through 1917 with a 5:17.0 – a world long course best — to his credit in that last year before he entered the military. Ranked just behind him was his countryman, Norman Ross, fresh from his Inter Allied Games victories in 1919 and who set a short course world mark of 5:14.6 later that year. None of the previous Olympic medalists except Frank Beaurepaire from Melbourne, Australia appeared to be a threat.

Georges Vernot from Montreal, Canada was the fastest heat winner with a 5:32.6 over Fred Kahele of the US Navy (5:37.6). Earlier Ross had swum only 6:16.2 in the first heat. Langer took the last one from Hodgson of Canada, the 1912 champion, by more than eight seconds with a 5:41.4. There were two close races in the semis, as Ross beat Kahele in the first, 5:33.8 to 5:35.8. In the second semi, Vernot swam away from Langer and Beaurepaire, a 1908 medal winner from Australia, with times of 5:27.8, 5:29.2 and 5:32.8, respectively.

Norman Ross (USA) earned double gold, winning the 400 and 1500-meter freestyle.

Ross raced through the first two hundred meters of the final in 2:32.4 to build an insurmountable lead. He won in 5:26.6, with Langer edging Vernot for second, 5:29.2 to 5:29.8.

Men's 1500 Meter Freestyle: Although Ludy Langer was the best 1500 meter and one-mile freestyler in 1915 -1916, he never regained his top form for the 1920 Games. Norman Ross appeared to be the co-favorite along with 1908 medalist Frank Beaurepaire. Both men had recorded times of just over 24 minutes in the mile after the war. This gave them a chance to better George Hodgson's world and Olympic 1500 mark from 1912.

Ross started slowly, clocking a modest 24:08.2 to qualify seventh. Beaurepaire led the field with his 22:55.0. Ross bounced back to win the first semifinal over U.S. Navy swimmers Fred Kahele and Eugene Bolden, the national AAU champion in the mile, in an extremely close race 23:22.6 to 23:25.0 and 23:26.4. Vernot nipped Beaurepaire in the second semi, 22:59.4 to 23:02.2.

In the final, Ross stormed from behind to pass Vernot and win by a large margin in 22:23.2, dismissing the Canadian (22:36.4) and Beaurepaire (23:04.0) with deceptive ease. The winning time was the fastest since the 1912 Games.

Warren Kealoha, part of the powerful Hawaiian contingent, took the 100-meter backstroke, setting a world record of 1:14.8 in the semifinals.

Men's 100 Meter Backstroke: Since most of the leading swimming nations did not hold a 100 meter backstroke event at their summer nationals, it was difficult to project a clear picture of the top Olympic contenders in advance. In 1918, Harold "Stubby" Kruger from Hui Nalu in Honolulu had slashed three seconds off the world long course best of Harry Hebner from 1912 with a 1:17.2 in Chicago. At the 1920 Pacific Coast Trials, Warren Kealoha from the Hui Makani Club in Honolulu further dropped the long course world best to 1:15.0 to establish himself as the Olympic favorite. Perry McGillivray, a national champion from the Illinois AC and a 1912 Games freestyle finalist, had set a world mark for 150 yards backstroke at the USA Indoor nationals in Indianapolis in May 1920. This trio plus Ray Kegeris of the Los Angeles AC gave the Americans high hopes of dominating this stroke at the Antwerp Games.

With a short, but wide body, Kealoha became the new master of Olympic and world backstroke in Antwerp. After setting a world and Olympic record of 1:14.8 for the 100 meter dorsal event in the preliminaries, he went on to take the final in 1:15.2. His new mark was six seconds faster than Hebner's 1912 world and Olympic best as well as two seconds faster than the world long course standard set by Stubby Kruger from 1918.

Kegeris (USA) beat Gerard Blitz from Brussels, Belgium, 1:16.2 to 1:19.0 for the silver medal. McGillivray was a close fourth in 1:19.4.

Men's 200 Meter Breaststroke: With the Germans not competing in Antwerp, the Swedes, untouched by war, boasted the strongest gold medal prospects in Hakan Malmroth and Thor Henning, their national champions of the two preceding years. Ivan Stedman (AUS) and Americans Mike McDermott, of the Illinois AC, and Jack Howell, from the Oakland AC, comprised the next tier of hopefuls.

At the Games, Malmroth swam to victory over teammate Henning, a Stockholm Games silver medalist in the 400 meter breast, with times of 3:04.0 in the heats, 3:09.0 in the semis and 3:04.4 in the final. Henning easily bested Finland's Arvo Aaltonen for the silver medal, with a 3:09.2 to the Finn's 3:12.2. Howell, who had won his heat in 3:09.8 and his semi in 3:10.8, could manage only a fourth in the final, with Stedman fifth.

Hakan Malmrot led a one-two Swedish sweep in both the 200- and 400-meter breaststroke – the only men's events in Antwerp the US failed to win.

Men's 400 Meter Breaststroke: Just as they were in the 200 meter breaststroke, the Swedish veterans, Hakan Malmroth and Thor Henning, several times national champions, were also favored in the longer event of this stroke. Malmroth led throughout the heats and semis, albeit by close margins: 6:49.0 to 6:50.0 over Arvo Aaltonen (FIN) and 6:44.8 to 6:45.6 over Per Cederholm, from Sweden's SKK Club, respectively. But those who smelled an upset in the final were quickly disappointed, as Malmroth took the lead at the start and kept extending it with every stroke, finishing nearly 13-1/2 seconds ahead of Henning in 6:31.8 to his teammate's 6:45.2. Aaltonen took his second bronze with a 6:49.0, two seconds ahead of the USA's Jack Howell. Walther Bathe's Olympic record of 6:29.6 from 1912 remained intact, as did his 200-meter breaststroke standard of 3:01.8.

Men's 4 x 200 Meter Freestyle Relay: The USA was an overwhelming favorite to win the 4x200 meter freestyle relay because of its great depth and the quality of its 100-400 meter freestylers. The likes of Kahanamoku, McGillivray, Wallen, Ross, Kealoha, Langer and Giebel were all fast and experienced in relay racing.

The relay produced a twenty-one second margin of victory by the USA over Australia, 10:04.4 to 10:25.4. The winning time was also more than seven seconds faster than Australasia's winning time in Stockholm eight years earlier. Great Britain, the 1908 champion, was a remote third in 10:37.1. The American quartet of Perry McGillivray, Pua Kealoha, Norman Ross and Duke Kahanamoku averaged 2:31.1, with McGillivray turning in the fastest split with a leadoff 2:27.2.

The USA men's 4 x 200-meter freestyle relay took the gold medal by a whopping 21 seconds over second-place Australia. From left: Ross, Kealoha, McGillivray, and Kahanamoku.

1920 WOMEN'S EVENTS

In the women's contests, nearly all of the competitors were virtually unknown outside of their own countries. With five years of NAAU Indoor and Outdoor meets under their belts and with no war-time suffering, the American women were ready to explode onto the Olympic scene in Antwerp. The addition of the 300 meter free to the 1920 program was a nice bonus for the USA since the best post-war 200 and 400 meter freestylers were American.

Women's 100 Meter Freestyle: In 1919, Charlotte Boyle (USA) from the WSA of New York, equaled Fanny Durack's 1915 long course world record of 1:16.2. Just two months before the Antwerp Games, at the Western USA Olympic Tryouts in Alameda, Caifornia, Frances Schroth (USA) from the Oakland AC dropped that standard down to 1:15.0. One month later, Ethelda Bleibtrey of the WSA destroyed that mark with an incredible 1:12.8 at the Eastern USA Tryouts at Manhattan Beach, N.Y.. With this trio plus Irene Guest from the Meadowbrook Club of Philadelphia, the American women were poised to sweep the 100 at the Antwerp Games.

This second edition of the Olympic 100 meter freestyle did turn out to be an all-American contest, as the USA contingent qualified 1-2-3-4 in the heats and finished 1-2-3-7 in the final. Bleibtrey won as she pleased in both the preliminary (1:14.4) and final (1:13.6). Far behind were her teammates, Guest in 1:17.0 and Schroth in 1:17.2. No other swimmer was able to better 1:20. The gold medal performance was more than seven seconds under Fanny Durack's 1912 world and Olympic record. It is surprising that such

The USA's Ethelda Bleibtrey was untouchable in Antwerp, winning three gold medals and leading one-two-three American sweeps of both the 100- and 300-meter freestyle events.

progress could occur in only a few years, especially with most of the world either fighting the most horrific war in history or preoccupied with avoiding being sucked into the conflagration during most of those years. The probable main causes for this great improvement were the entry of America into the sport on a national and international level, the great changes in stroke technique – particularly the changeover from trudgeon to crawl – plus some excellent coaching.

Women's 300 Meter Freestyle: Ethelda Bleibtrey entered the new 300-meter event as the probable winner because of her excellent pre-Olympic swimming over 100 and 400 meters. At the latter distance, she was indisputably the best in the world with a long course 6:21.6 in Honolulu in April of the Olympic year. Margaret Woodbridge, the USA Indoor champion at 500 yards, was another strong contender.

As in the 100 meter free, Bleibtrey took early command of this new Olympic event to win by nearly nine seconds in world record time of 4:34.0 –almost 10 seconds faster than Fanny Durack's mark from 1912. The distant silver medalist, Margaret Woodbridge from Detroit, was also under the previous world best with a 4:42.2. Frances Schroth made it another American sweep by touching out Britain's Connie Jeans in 4:52.0 to 4:52.4.

Women's 4 x 100 Meter Freestyle Relay: No other country could match the United States' speed or depth. As expected, the USA captured the women's relay over Great Britain and Sweden. The winning time of 5:11.6 was more than 10 seconds faster per leg than Britain's world best of 5:52.8 from the 1912 Games. The victorious quartet of Ethelda Bleibtrey, Irene Guest, Frances Schroth and Margaret Woodbridge finished nearly 20 seconds ahead of a vastly improved British team that beat Sweden for the silver medal, 5:40.8 to 5:43.6.

In this first great meeting of the post-war world, the United States established itself as the world's greatest swimming power. With strong Amateur Athletic Union (AAU) clubs and with widespread and developing high school and university swimming programs the U.S. would maintain its number one ranking in the sport for most of the next nine decades, with the exception of a few lean periods.

The victorious U.S. women's 4 x 100m-freestyle relay was more than 20 seconds quicker than second-place Great Britain. From Left: Schroth, Woodbridge, Bleibtrey, and Guest.

1920 OLYMPIC SWIMMING RESULTS
ANTWERP, BELGIUM
100 METER COURSE

Men's 100 Meter Freestyle:		Trial		Semi		Final	Reswim
1) Duke Kahanamoku	USA	Lo1:01.8	I	Lo1:01.4	I	Lo1:00.4	1:01.4
2) Pu Kealoha	USA	1:02.0	III	1:02.4	II	1:02.2	1:02.6
3) William Harris	USA	1:04.4	VI	1:04.8	I	1:03.2	1:03.0
4 William Herald	AUS	1:05.6	V	1:05.8	II	No Time	1:03.8
Norman Ross	USA	1:04.4	V	1:04.8	II	1:03.8	DNS
Georges Vernot	CAN	1:05.2	IV	1:05.8	I		
Ivan Stedman	AUS	1:04.2	III	No Time	II		
Ko Korsten	NED	1:05.6	VI	No Time	II		
Harry Hay	AUS	1:06.2	IV	No Time	I		
Orvar Trolle	SWE	1:07.2	IV	No Time	II		
K. Kirkland	AUS	1:08.0	I	No Time	II		
Henri Padou	FRA	1:08.4	III				
Jean van Silfhout	NED	1:09.0	I				
J. Dickson	GBR	1:10.o	VI				
Mario Massa	ITA	1:10.4	V				
Agostino Frassinetti	ITA	1:11.8	II	No Time	I		
V. Buchacek	CZE	1:19.2	II	No Time	I		
A. Gammaro	BRA	1:22.o	II				
Georges Pouilley	FRA	No Time	I				
Albert Dickin	GBR	No Time	I				
Harold Annison	GBR	No Time	II				
Martial van Schelle	BEL	No Time	III				
Jean Jenni	SUI	No Time	III				
Kenkichi Saito	JPN	No Time	III				
Leon Pesch	LUX	No Time	IV				
Leslie Savage	GBR	No Time	IV				
Orlando Armendola	BRA	No Time	IV				
Gerard Blitz	BEL	No Time	V				

Men's 400 Meter Freestyle		Trial		Semi		Final
1) Norman Ross	USA	6:16.2	I	5:33.8	I	5:26.8
2) Ludy Langer	USA	5:41.4	V	5:29.2	II	5:29.2
3) Georges Vernot	CAN	5:32.6	IV	5:27.8	II	5:29.8
4 Fred Kahele	USA	5:37.6	IV	5:35.8	I	No Time
Frank Beaurepaire	AUS	5:42.0	IV	5:32.8	II	DNF
William Harris	USA	5:57.8	III	5:36.0	I	
George Hodgson	CAN	5:49.8	V	No Time	II	
Jack Hatfield	GBR	5:50.6	V			
Harold Annison	GBR	5:56.0	II	No Time	II	
Henry Taylor	GBR	6:01.2	III	No Time	I	
Kieth Kirkland	AUS	6:12.2	II	DNF	II	
Kane Kichi Saitoh	JPN	6:16.8	I	DNF	I	
Paul Vasseur	FRA	6:30.4	II			
Albert Steen	NOR	6:30.6	II			

Seiren Uchida	JPN	6:40.0	III				
Rene Ricxolfi-DSoria	SUI	No Time	II				
Alois Hrasek	CZE	No Time	III				
Arne Borg	SWE	No Time	IV				
Percy Peter	GBR	No Time	IV				
Gilio Bisagno	ITA	No Time	IV				
Harry Hay	AUS	No Time	V				
Antonio Quarantotto	ITA	No Time	V				

Men's 1500 Meter Freestyle:

		Trial		Semi		Final
1) Norman Ross	USA	24:08.3	IV	23:12.0	I	22:23.2
2) Georges Vernot	CAN	23:40.0	I	22:59.4	II	22:36.4
3) Frank Beaurepaire	AUS	22:55.4	V	23:02.2	II	23:00.4
4 Fred Kahele	USA	23:41.6	V	23:25.0	I	No Time
Eugene Bolden	USA	23:41.2	I	23:26.4	I	
Harold Annison	GBR	24:28.2	III	23:51.4	II	
Jack Hatfield	GBR	23:46.4	V			
Arnee Borg	SWE	23:54.4	I	No Time	I	
Ludy Langer	USA	23:28.8	II	No Time	II	
George Hodgson	CAN	24:36.6	III	No Time	I	
Percy Peter	GBR	24:39.4	II	No Time	II	
Cor Zegger	NED	24:58.0	II			
Giglio Bisagno	ITA	25:18.0	III			
Paul DeBacker	BEL	26:46.4	IV	No Time	II	
Frans Moller	SWE	27:42.4	IV			
Antonio Quarantotto	ITA	No Time	II			
Alois Hrasek	CZE	No Time	II			
++ Hans Drexler	SUI	No Time	III			
Emanuel Prull	CZE	No Time	III			
Joachim C. Esquerra	ESP	No Time	IV			
Henry Taylor	GBR	DNF	I			
Rene Ricolfi-Doria	SUI	DNF	I			
Pierre Lavraie	FRA	DNF	V			

Men's 100 Meter Backstroke:

		Trial		Final
1) Warren Kealoha	USA	WLo1:14.8	II	1:15.2
2) Ray Kegeris	USA	o1:17.8	I	1:16.2
3) Gerard Blitz	BEL	1:18.6	II	1:19.0
4 Perry McGillivray	USA	1:20.4	II	1:19.4
5 Harold Kruger	USA	1:19.0	I	No Time
Per Holmstrom	SWE	1:26.0	II	
Gaspard Lemaire	BEL	1:28.0	I	
Asborn Wang	NOR	1:28.2	I	
Geoege Webster	GBR	No Time	II	
Henri Matter	FRA	No Time	I	
George Robertson	GBR	No Time	I	
Daniel Lehu	FRA	No Time	II	

Men's 200 Meter Breaststroke:

			Trial		Semi		Final
1)	Hakan Malmroth	SWE	3:04.0	III	3:09.0	I	3:04.4
2)	Thor Henning	SWE	3:12.8	IV	3:16.0	II	3:09.2
3)	Arvo Aaltonen	FIN	3:11.6	III	3:12.4	I	3:12.2
4	Jack Howell	USA	3:09.8	I	3:10.8	II	No Time
5	Ivan Stedman	AUS	3:18.8	IV	3:16.0	I	No Time
	Per Cederholm	SWE	3:12.2	I	3:14.6	I	DNF
	Olle Dickson	SWE	3:16.0	II	No Time	I	
	Mike McDermott	USA	3:16.4	II	No Time	II	
	Paul Neeckx	BEL	3:16.6	II	No Time	I	
	Edouard Henry	BEL	3:18.0	I			
	William Stoney	GBR	3:20.8	IV			
	E. van Hoelen	BEL	3:22.6	III			
	Rex Lassam	GBR	No Time	I			
	Sydney Gooday	CAN	No Time	I			
	Theodore Michel	LUX	No Time	II			
	Emile Arbogast	FRA	No Time	II			
	Ernest Parker	GBR	No Time	II			
	Stephen Ruddy	USA	No Time	III			
	Eduard Stibor	CZE	No Time	III			
	George Robertson	GBR	No Time	III			
	Herbert Taylor	USA	No Time	IV			
+	Andre Lebaillif	FRA	No Time	IV			
	Luis Balcells Auter	ESP	No Time	IV			
	Felicien Courbet	BEL	No Time	IV			

Men's 400 Meter Breaststroke:

			Trial		Semi		Final
1)	Hakan Malmroth	SWE	6:49.0	II	6:44.8	I	6:31.8
2)	Thor Henning	SWE	6:46.2	I	6:45.0	II	6:45.2
3)	Arvo Aaltonen	FIN	6:50.0	II	6:45.0	II	6:48.0
4	Jack Howell	USA	6:57.0	III	6:51.0	II	6:51.0
	Per Cederholm	SWE	7:14.0	III	6:45.6	I	No Time
	Olle Dickson	SWE	7:12.0	IV	6:59.o	II	
	Mike McDermott	USA	7:12.8	I	7:13.2	I	
	Andre Lebaillif	FRA	7:12.2	I	No Time	II	
	Henri Demieville	SUI	7:12.4	IV	No Time	I	
	Steve Ruddy	USA	7:13.0	IV			
	Felicien Courbet	BEL	7:20.0	II			
	George Robertson	GBR	7:28.0	III			
	Rex Lassam	GBR	No Time	I			
	Charles Quimby	GBR	No Time	II			
	Emile Arbogast	FRA	No Time	III			
	Edouard Henry	BEL	No Time	III			
	Edouard van Haelen	BEL	No Time	IV			
	Eduard Stibor	CZE	No Time	IV			
	Sydney Gooday	CAN	DNF	I			
	Luis Bacells Auter	ESP	DNF	II			

Men's 4x200 Meter Freestyle:	Trial		Final
2:27.2 2:33.2 2:30.0 2:34.0			
1) USA (McGillivray,P.Kealoha,Ross,Kahanamoku)	10:20.4	I	Lo10:04.4
2) AUS (Hay,Herald,Stedman,Beaurepaire)	10:36.4	I	10:25.4
3) GBR (Savage,Peter,Taylor,Annison)	10:51.0	II	10:37.2
4 SWE (R.Andersson,Moller,Trolle,Arne Borg)	10:54.4	I	10:50.2
5 ITA (Massa,Frassinetti,Quarantotto,Bisagno)	11:01.2	II	No Time
BEL (Vermetten,Cludrs,Bauwens,Blitz)	11:12.2	II	
FRA (Mayaud,Vasseur,Pouilley,Padou)	11:53.0	I	

For Australia, Beaurepaire swam for Kirkland in the final

1920 Men's Olympic Swimming Medals

	Gold	Medals
USA	5	9
SWE	2	4
AUS	0	2
CAN	0	2
FIN	0	2
BEL	0	1
GBR	0	1

1896–1920 Men's Olympic Swimming Medals

	Gold	Medals
USA	10	26
GER	8	17
GBR	6	15
HUN	4	11
AUS	3	10
SWE	2	7
CAN	2	4
AUT	1	8
FRA	1	4
GRE	0	5
DEN	0	2
FIN	0	2
BEL	0	1
NED	0	1

Women's 100 Meter Freestyle:		Trial		Final
1) Ethelda Bleibtrey	USA	Wo1:14.4	III	o1:13.6
2) Irene Guest	USA	1:18.8	II	1:17.0
3) Frances Schroth	USA	o1:18.0	I	1:17.2
4 Constance Jeans	GBR	1:20.8	II	1:22.8
5 Violet Walrand	NZL	1:21.4	II	No Time
6 Jane Gylling	SWE	1:25.6	III	No Time
7 Charlotte Boyle	USA	1:20.4	I	DNF
Marie Beisenherz	NED	1:22.6	I	
Grace McKenzie	GBR	1:27.4	III	
Yvonne Degraine	FRA	No Time	I	
Aina Berg	SWE	No Time	I	
Lillian Birkenhead	GBR	No Time	I	
Germaine van Dievoet	BEL	No Time	II	
Suzanne Wurtz	FRA	No Time	II	
Carin Nilsson	SWE	No Time	II	
Charlotte Radcliffe	GBR	No Time	II	
Ernestine Lebrun	FRA	No Time	III	

| Barbara"Blanche"Nash | SAF | No Time III |
| Lily Beaurepaire | AUS | No Time III |

Women's 300 Meter Freestyle:		Trial			Final
1) Ethelda Bleibtrey	USA	4:41.4	I		4:34.0
2) Margaret Woodbridge	USA	4:56.6	II		4:42.4
3) Frances Schroth	USA	5:03.2	III		4:52.0
4 Constance Jeans	GBR	4:59.8	I		4:52.4
5 Eleanor Uhl	USA	5:02.0	III		No Time
Jane Gylling	SWE	5:04.8	II		No Time
Carin Nilsson	SWE	5:07.0	I		No Time
Violet Walrond	NZL	5:04.6	II		No Time
Hilda James	GBR	5:07.2	I		
Aina Berg	SWE	5:29.6	III		
Suzanne Wurtz	FRA	5:33.0	III		
Lily Beaurepaire	AUS	No Time	I		
Grace McKenzie	GBR	No Time	II		
Ernestine Lebrun	FRA	No Time	II		
Florence Sancroft	GBR	No Time	III		
Barbara"Blanche"Nash	SAF	No Time	III		

Women's 4x100 Meter Freestyle Relay:	Final
1) USA (Bleibtrey,Guest,Schroth,Woodbridge)	Lo5:11.6
2) GBR (Radcliffe,James,McKenzie,Jeans)	5:40.8
3) SWE (Macknow,Berg,Gylling,Nilsson)	5:43.6

W World Record, L Long Course Best, o Olympic Record

1920 Women's Olympic Swimming Medals   1896-1920 Women's Olympic Swimming Medals

	Gold	Medals		Gold	Medals
USA	3	7	USA	3	7
GBR	0	1	GBR	1	3
SWE	0	1	AUS	1	2
			GER	0	1
			SWE	0	1
			AUT	0	1

1924: Paris, France
(50 Meter Pool, Fresh Water)

Start of the men's 100-meter freestyle at the Piscine des Tourelles, site of the aquatic events at the 1924 Olympic Games in Paris.

For the first time ever, the aquatic events of the Olympic Games took place in a modern swimming stadium: the "Piscine des Tourelles"— since renamed the "Stade Georges Vallerey." This great center is still the site of major swimming competitions as well as the offices of the French Swimming Federation.

For the 1924 Games, FINA, swimming's international governing body, reduced the length of the Olympic course from 100 meters to 50 meters and introduced lane lines to prevent collisions. Even though the unheated water was chilly, the shorter pool length and lane lines helped make for faster performances at these second Paris Games.

As they had four years earlier, the Americans arrived at the Games with a powerful and balanced team of men and women. The American men held four of six world records at Olympic distances as well as three of six world long course bests in these same events.

In men's freestyle, three post-war giants of swimming emerged from these 1924 Games: Johnny Weissmuller (USA) from the Illinois AC, Arne Borg (SWE) from SKK and Andrew "Boy" Charlton from Sydney Australia. Between 1921 and 1929, this mighty trio dominated men's Olympic swimming and completely rewrote the freestyle world record book with performances far above the level of the pre-war and the immediate post-war champions.

1924 MEN'S EVENTS

Men's 100 Meter Freestyle: Following his long course, salt-water world record of 58.6 for 100 meter freestyle in Alameda, California in 1922, Johnny Weissmuller, the tall, Austrian–American, established himself as the overwhelming favorite to win this event. The leading hopefuls for the other medals included 34 year-old Duke Kahanamoku, his brother, Sam, and Arne Borg.

Sam Kahanamoku led the field through the heats with a comfortable 1:03.2, with six others under 1:05.0. In the semifinals the real competition began. The Duke pulled out the first race with a 1:01.6 in a close finish over his brother, Sam (1:02.2). Katsuo Takaishi (JPN) and Orvar Trolle (SWE) were a touch behind at 1:02.4 and 1:02.6. Weissmuller easily won the second semi in 1:00.8, well ahead of Borg (1:02.6) and Australia's Ernest Henry (1:03.0).

In the final, Weissmuller took command at the start, turning in a fast 27.6 at the 50, then leading a USA sweep with a 59.0 — 1.4 seconds under the 1920 Olympic mark of the Duke, who finished second in 1:01.4, just ahead of his younger brother, Sam (1:01.8). Borg was a close fourth in 1:02.0. In fifth was Takaishi (1:03.0), the first Japanese to reach an Olympic final.

Swimming in his first Olympic Games in 1924, Johnny Weissmuller dethroned 34 year-old Duke Kahanamoku in the 100 free before going on to win two additional gold medals.

Men's 400 Meter Freestyle: The metric quarter mile event brought Johnny Weissmuller, Arne Borg and Andrew "Boy" Charlton together for the first and only occasion in their Olympic careers. The American held the world record of 4:57.0, swum in a short course pool, and he also had swum a long course 5:06.6 in Hawaii two years earlier. But, in the spring of 1924, the slender Borg had posted a stunning world long course best time of 4:59.0 at the fast, salt-water course in Honolulu. Meanwhile, in Sydney, the powerful 18-year-old Charlton ensured his pre-Olympic co-favorite status by winning the 1924 New South Wales 440 yard title in 5:11.8 over a 55-yard salt-water course in Sydney. Realistically, no otter swimmer was given a chance of challenging this mighty trio.

In the heats, Weissmuller set an Olympic record as he cruised a 5:22.2, with his chief rivals both clocking over 5:30. In the first semifinal, the tall American crushed the Australian star by 19 seconds, lowering his Olympic mark to 5:13.6. Borg took the second semi in 5:21.4, beating his brother, Ake, by 3.6 seconds.

Then came the long-awaited final. Weissmuller and Borg virtually sprinted the first 100 meters, turning together in 1:04.2 with the slower Charlton trailing by about five meters. At the halfway mark, the two leaders had slowed down but still split a fast 2:23.0 as Charlton had dropped even farther back. By 300 meters, Borg had pulled ahead, turning with a slight lead in 3:45.5. But Weissmuller was not about to give up and the two rivals turned together with one length left to swim. Then Weissmuller uncorked a powerful finishing sprint to win in the Olympic record time of 5:04.2. Borg was just able to hold off the fast closing Charlton, 5:05.6 to 5:06.6. These three performances were all the more remarkable since no other swimmer had ever posted a long course time under 5:17.0. Ake Borg was a distant fourth ahead of the 1912 silver medalist, Jack Hatfield (GBR), 5:26.0 to 5:32.0.

Men's 1500 Meter Freestyle: Held earlier in the Olympic program than the 400 meter free, the 1500 shaped up as a likely contest between world record-holder Borg (21:15.0) and Charlton, the former 800 meter world record-holder.

With a rapid swim of 21:20.4 in the third heat, the young Australian destroyed George Hodgson's 1912 Olympic mark by nearly 40 seconds. As fast as it was, the new Olympic record lasted barely an hour. In the fourth heat, Sweden's Borg rose to the challenge, slashing nine full seconds off Charlton's mark with a speedy 21:11.4, a time that also lowered his own global standard.

The two favorites met in the first semifinal with Charlton finishing far ahead, 21:28.4 to 21:50.6. With a 21:53.4, Jack Hatfield was a strong third. Frank Beaurepaire, the 33 year-old veteran Australian, swam his fastest-ever 1500 to win the second semi in 21:41.6 over 100-meter finalist Katsuo Takaishi (21:48.6) and Ake Borg (21:59.4). In these semifinals no fewer than six men swam faster than Hodgson's world and Olympic record.

The 1500 meter final, billed as "the battle of the distance kings," lived up to expectations — for the first 400 meters. At that point, Charlton held a small lead

Australia's Andrew "Boy" Charlton destroyed the field in the 1500 meters. His time, 20:06.6, carved more than a minute off the pending world record by Sweden's Arne Borg, who finished second.

over Borg, as they turned in 5:10.4 and 5:11.0. Then Borg began to drop back as his rival continued his murderous pace to reach the 800 meter mark in 10:35.2, more than eight seconds under Borg's world record for the metric half mile. Charlton kept up the pace, splitting 13:19.6 at the1000-meter mark — an amazing 40 seconds faster than the Swede's world mark for that distance. At the finish, the powerful Australian touched in the incredible time of 20:06.6 – more than a minute faster than Borg's pending world record from the preliminaries, with the Swede far behind in 20:41.4, the second fastest time ever. Beaurepaire, the 1908 medalist from Melbourne, took the bronze medal in 21:48.4 over a minute behind Borg. Hatfield was fourth in 21:55.6, well ahead of Takaishi (22:10.4).

Warren Kealoha reprised his 1920 victory in the 100-meter backstroke, lowering his Olympic record to 1:13.2.

Men's 100 Meter Backstroke: Warren Kealoha showed the world that he was ready to defend his Olympic title by swimming the long course 100 meter backstroke in 1:13.6 in October 1923 and 1:12.4 in April of 1924 in Honolulu, both well under his 1920 winning time of 1:14.8 in 1920. Karoly Bartha (HUN), from the NSC club, Osamu Oeda (JPN), Gerard Blitz (BEL) the bronze medalist in 1920, and English ASA champion, Austin Rawlinson, appeared to be the main contenders for the other medals.

Kealoha, of the Hui Makani Club in Hawaii, was far ahead of the field on all three rounds. His times of 1:13.4, 1:13.6 and 1:13.2 in the heat, semi and final, although well behind his own world and long course best time of 1:12.4, were still far ahead of the rest of the world. Little-known Paul Wyatt (USA) from Uniontown, Pennsylvania, won the silver meal in 1:15.4, comfortably ahead of Bartha (1:17.8). Blitz edged Rawlinson for fourth, 1:19.6 to 1:20.0.

Men's 200 Meter Breaststroke: Bob Skelton (USA) from the Illinois AC— briefly the world record-holder for the 200 meter breaststroke with a 2:52.6 in March of 1924 and boasting a long course best of 2:56.6 — was considered the man to beat in this Olympic event. Only Germany's Erich Rademacher, who had a long course best of 2:55.7 from 1922 and who lowered Skelton's world record to 2:50.4 in a 25-meter pool just one month after the Games, appeared to be in his class. Unfortunately, once again, in the aftermath of the Great War, the Germans were barred from competing.

In Rademacher's absence, Skelton won the Olympic 200 meter breaststroke final handily. After setting a new Olympic mark of 2:56.0 in the preliminary and coasting through his semifinal, he came back to capture the final in 2:56.6. Joseph de Combe

Sybil Bauer, the first woman to swim faster than the men's world record in an event (6:24 for 440 yards backstroke) won the 100 back in Paris by more than four seconds. Tragically, she died of cancer at 22.

Women's 100 Meter Backstroke: Prior to the 1924 Games, the USA's Sybil Bauer, from the Illinois AC, was the overwhelming favorite to win the new backstroke event. Her long course world record of 1:26.6 in 1923 was more than eight seconds under the old mark. At the USA Olympic Tryouts, she carved another four seconds off this time with an amazing 1:22.6. Earlier, she had swum a world record 1:22.4 in a short course pool. Before these 1924 Games, no other swimmer had even approached her pre–Games performances.

Bauer easily swam away with the Olympic title in the 100 meter backstroke, Her heat time of 1:24.0 and her winning performance of 1:23.2 placed her far ahead of the rest of the field. Britain's Phyllis Harding from the Croydon Ladies Club worked hard to hold off Aileen Riggin (USA), the 1920 springboard diving gold medalist from the Women's SA of New York, 1:27.4 to 1:28.2. The other finalists, Florence Chambers (USA) and Jarmilla Mullerova (CZE), were well astern in 1:30.4 and 1:31.2.

Great Britain's Lucy Morton prevented a U.S. gold medal sweep in Paris, out-sprinting American, Agnes Geraghty, to the wall in the 200-m breaststroke.

Women's 200 Meter Breaststroke

: Pre-Games predictions were extremely difficult in this first Olympic breaststroke event for women. Among those considered possible medalists were Agnes Geraghty (USA) from the WSA, Maria Baron (NED) from the ODZ Club plus Irene Gilbert and Doris Hart from Britain.

As it turned out, this event was full of surprises and some very fast swimming. In the first heat of the preliminaries, Maria Baron was disqualified on a turn after swimming 3:22.6, by far the fastest long course time ever. In this same heat, Geraghty touched in 3:27.6, six seconds under the American record and two seconds ahead of the rest of the field. Gilbert, from the Attercliffe Ladies Club and the world record-holder from 1923, finished second, but her 3:32.8 left her more than five seconds behind the American. The second and third prelim heats were won handily by the other two British entries, Lucy Morton from Blackpool SC and Gladys Carson from the Leicester Ladies Club, in 3:29.4 and 3:30.0, respectively.

After these very fast heats, the final turned out to be a stirring contest with remarkably slow finishing times. Geraghty led for the first 150 meters before she was caught and passed by Morton. Over the last length there was a hard-fought, three-way struggle to the finish, with Morton beating the American, 3:33.2 to 3:34.0. Carson was a close third in 3:35.4. Gilbert, the world record-holder, could manage only a fifth in 3:38.0, four-tenths of a second behind Sweden's Vivian Pettersson.

Women's 4 x 100 Meter Freestyle Relay: With the three 100-meter freestyle medalists plus the fifth-fastest swimmer of the Olympic year, an American victory in the relay was all but assured. And so it came to pass. The winning team of Ederle, Euphrasia Donnelly, Lackie and Wehselau finished in an Olympic record and world long course best of 4:58.8, hacking 12.2 seconds off the former mark set four years earlier by the American team in Antwerp. Britain was a distant second in 5:17.0, well ahead of third place Sweden's 5:35.6.

Even though the USA dominated the top places in the women's events in Paris, with four out of five gold medals plus five other medals, the British performed extremely well with one title and with seven different swimmers earning Olympic medals.

1924 OLYMPIC SWIMMING RESULTS
PARIS, FRANCE-OUTDOOR 50 METER POOL

Men's 100 Meter Freestyle:

			Trial		Semi		Final
1)	John Weissmuller	USA	1:03.8	V	1:00.8	II	o59.0
2)	Duke Kahanamoku	USA	1:04.3	I	1:01.6	I	1:01.4
3)	Sam Kahanamoku	USA	1;03.2	II	1:02.2	I	1:01.8
4	Arne Borg	SWE	1:05.4	VI	1:02.6	II	1:02.0
5	Katsuo Takaishi	JPN	1:04.0	IV	1:02.4	I	1:03.0
6	Orvar Trolle	SWE	1:04.2	I	1:02.6	I	No Time
	Ernest Henry	AUS	1:03.8	II	1:03.0	II	
	Alfred Pycock	GBR	1:05.2	V	1:05.0	II	
	Clayton Bourne	CAN	1:06.2	III	1:06.0	I	
	Ivan Stedman	AUS	1:06.0	IV	1:06.4	II	
	Victoriano Zorilla	ARG	1:08.2	III	1:07.6	II	
	Torahiko Miyahata	JPN	1:04.2	II			
	Henri Padou	FRA	1:05.0	II			
	Kasuo Onoda	JPN	1:05.4	I			
	Albert Dicken	GBR	1:06.0	II			
	Eduard Vanzeveren	FRA	1:06.8	V			
	Georg Werner	SWE	1:07.0	IV			
	Moss Christie	AUS	1:07.2	V			
	Emil Zeibig	FRA	1:08.0	IV			
	Charles Baillee	GBR	1:08.2	I			
	Istvan Barany	HUN	1:08.4	VI			
	S. Bicak	CZE	1:10,2	II			
	V. Smokvina	YUG	1:11.6	I			
	G. Dekker	NED	1:11.8	IV			
	J. Balaz	CZE	1:11.8	VI			
	Denis Vassilopoulos	GRE	1:12.0	VI			
	P. Jacobszoon	NED	1:12.2	VI			
	V. Legat	CZE	1:13.2	III			
	J. Pinillo	ESP	1:14.2	V			
	C. Kopp	SUI	1:15.0	III			

Men's 400 Meter Freestyle:

			Trial		Semi		Final
1)	John Weissmuller	USA	o5:22.2	III	o5:13.6	I	o5:04.2
2)	Arne Borg	SWE	5:31.8	IV	5:21.4	II	5:05.6
3)	Andrew "Boy" Charlton	AUS	5:30.2	III	5:32.6	I	5:06.6
4	Ake Borg	SWE	5:28.2	II	5:25.0	II	5:26.0
5	John Hatfield	GBR	5:32.6	I	5:30.4	II	5:32.0
	Lester Smith	USA	5:32.4	V	5:37.4	I	
	Georges Vernot	CAN	5:35.2	V	5:38.0	I	
	Harold Annison	GBR	5:32.6	V	5:39.4	II	
	Vaclav Antos	CZE	5:34.8	II	5:53.2	I	
	Ralph Breyer	USA	o5:22.4	I	Withdrew		
	Geoeges Vernot	CAN	5:35.2	V			
	Frank Beaurepaire	AUS	5:38.0	IV			
	Percy Peter	GBR	5:38.6	III			

Moss Christie	AUS	5:39.2	I			
Kasuo Onoda	JPN	5:43.8	IV			
Victoriano Zorilla	ARG	5:49.4	IV			
S. Bicak	CZE	5:52.4	IV			
S. Pellegry	FRA	5:56.2	III			
Eduard Vanzeveren	FRA	5:59.8	V			
Ko Kohler	NED	6:20.4	III			
Denis Vassibopoulos	GRE	6:21.4	II			
Pedro Mendez	ESP	6:26.6	V			
A. Venturini	YUG	6:28.4	I			
D. Sendjerdji	YUG	6:41.4	II			

Men's 1500 Meter Freestyle:

		Trial		Semi		Final
1) Andrew "Boy" Charlton	AUS	Lo21:20.4 III		21:28.4	I	Wo20:06.6
2) Arne Borg	SWE	Lo21:11.4 IV		21:50.6	I	20:41.4
3) Frank Beaurepaire	AUS	22:17.6	V	21:41.6	II	21:48.4
4 Jack Hatfield	GBR	22:26.8	III	21:53.4	I	21:55.6
5 Katsuo Takaishi	JPN	22:43.2	IV	21:48.6	II	22:10.4
Ake Borg	SWE	22:55.2	II	21:59.4	II	
Adam Smith	USA	22:48.8	I	22:39.8	I	
Georges Vernot	CAN	23:11.4	V	23:02.4	I	
Harold Annison	GBR	22:38.4	I	23:11.8	II	
John Taylor	GBR	23:16.6	II	23:13.8	I	
Dick Howell	USA	22:48.2	III	DNS		
Moss Christy	AUS	DQ22:49.4 I		DNS		
J. Taylor	GBR	23:16.6	II			
Kasuo Noda	JPN	23:44.2	II			
Salvator Pellegry	FRA	24:07.6	V			
Vaclav Antos	CZE	24:44.0	V			
Pedro Mendez	ESP	26:23.5	V			
Jean Rebeyrol	FRA	24:46.4	II			
Renato Bacigalupo	ITA	25:04.4	IV			
Denis Vassilopoulos	GRE	26:17.4	III			
G. Klein	FRA	DNF	I			
Kasuo Onoda	JPN	DNF	I			
A. Roje	YUG	DNF	III			

Men's 100 Meter Backstroke:

		Trial		Semi		Final
1) Warren Kealoha	USA	o1:13.4	I	1:13.6	I	o1:13.2
2) Paul Wyatt	USA	1:19.4	III	1:17.0	I	1:15.4
3) Karoly Bartha	HUN	1:18.4	II	1:19.4	I	1:17.8
4 Gerard Blitz	BEL	1:19.6	I	1:19.2	II	1:19.6
5 Austin Rawlinson	GBR	1:18.8	IV	1:19.2	II	1:20.0
Takahiro Saitoh	JPN	1:20.2	IV	1:19.6	I	
John MacDowell	GBR	1:21.8	II	1:22.0	I	
Erik Skoglund	SWE	1:27.4	V	1:22.6	I	
Emile Zeibig	FRA	1:22.4	III	1:23.6	II	
James Worthington	GBR	1:23.2	I	1:24.2	II	

Sven Thaulow	NOR	1:24.0	V	1:24.3 II	
Aart van Wilgenburg	NED	1:24.6	II		
Pieter van Senus	NED	1:24.8	IV		
Maurice Ducos	FRA	1:25.0	I		
T. Ishida	JPN	1:26.0	II		
Victor Legat	CZE	1:27.8	V		
G. Paulus	FRA	1:28.0	II		
Eugene Kuborn	LUX	1:29.0	V		
JP Moris	LUX	1:41.2	III		
H. Luning	USA	DQ1:16.4	II		

Men's 200 Meter Breaststroke:		Trial		Semi		Final
1) Robert Skelton	USA	o2:56.0	I	3:00.2	I	2:56.6
2) Joseph de Combe	BEL	3:02.0	II	3:00.2	II	2:59.2
3) William Kirchbaum	USA	3:01.0	III	3:02.2	I	3:01.0
4 Bengt Linders	SWE	3:03.4	V	3:01.4	II	3:02.2
5 Robert Wyss	SUI	3:03.6	V	3:04.2	I	3:03.3
Thor Henning	SWE	3:02.4	I	3:05.0	II	
Frederic Hollosy	HUN	3:06.4	IV	3:05.6	I	
Reg Flint	GBR	3:05.2	IV	3:06.8	I	
Edward Maw	GBR	3:07.0	II	3:07.0	II	
Zoltan Bitskey	HUN	3:05.4	I	3:09.2	II	
Rudolph Piovaty	CZE	3:10.8	III	3:11.8	I	
Ivan Stedman	AUS	3:05.6	I			
Henri Bouvier	FRA	3:07.8	IV			
Ernest Heard	NZL	3:09.0	V			
Tsunebu Ischida	JPN	3:09.2	V			
Martin Sipos	HUN	3:09.8	II			
William Stoney	GBR	3:10.3	I			
Arvo Aaltonen	FIN	3:11.0	II			
Georges Vallerey	FRA	3:11.2	I			
Marius Zwiller	FRA	3:11.2	II			
Bo Johnsson	SWE	3:12.2	III			
Viljo Viklund	FIN	3:12.4	III			
Gerlaous Moes	NED	3:18.8	IV			
Jaroslav Muller	CZE	3:22.0	V			
Luciano Trolli	ITA	3:23.0	III			
Emerico Balach	ITA	3:26.8	IV			
Ivo Pavelic	YUG	3:28.4	IV			
Mario da Silva Marques	POR	3:32.4	V			

Men's 4x200 Meter Freestyle Relay:	Trial		Semi		Final
1) USA (O'Connor,Glancy,Breyer,Weissmuller)	10:41.6	I	Lo9:59.4	II	Lo9:53.4
2) AUS (Christie,Henry,Beaurepaire,Charlton)	10:21.2	III	10:27.0	I	10:02.2
3) SWE (Werner,Trolle,Ake Borg,Arne Borg)	10:15.4	II	10:08.2	II	10:06.8
4 JPN (Miyahata,Takaishi,Noda,Onoda)	10:24.2	III	10:12.4	II	10:16.2
5 GBR (Thomson,Dicken,Annison,Peter)	10:52.3	IV	10:31.2	I	10:29.4
FRA (Padou,Vanzeveren,Middleton,Zeibig)	10:41.4	IV	10:39.4	II	

ITA (Bacigalupo,Frassinetti,Patrignani,Polli)   11:05.2 I   11:00.4 I
NED (Dekker,Hoogesteyn,Kohler,Schutte)   11:35.6 II   11:29.0 I
CZE (Antos,Blcak,LeGat,Piovati)   11:12.8 III
BEL (Buydens,Callens,Theinpondt,van Schelle)   11:14.8 IV
YUG (Arcanin,Roje,Smokvina,Venturini)   12:02.4 I
ESP (Berdenas,Mendez,Peredejordi,Pinello)   12:21.2 I

In the prelims, R.Howell swam in place of Weissmuller (USA), Stedman for Charlton (AUS), Henning and Persson for Ake and Arne Borg (SWE).

1924 Men's Olympic Swimming Medals		
	Gold	Medals
USA	5	9
AUS	1	4
SWE	0	3
HUN	0	1
BEL	0	1

1896–1924 Men's Olympic Swimming Medals		
	Gold	Medals
USA	15	35
GER	8	17
GBR	6	15
AUS	4	14
HUN	4	12
SWE	2	10
CAN	2	4
AUT	1	8
FRA	1	4
GRE	0	5
DEN	0	2
FIN	0	2
NED	0	1
BEL	0	2

Women's 100 Meter Freestyle:		Trial		Semi		Final
1) Ethel Lackie	USA	1:12.8	II	1:16.0 I		1:12.4
2) Mariechen Wehselau	USA	wo1:12.2 I		1:15.2 I		1:12.8
3) Gertrude Ederle	USA	1:12.6	III	1:15.4 II		1:14.2
4 Constance Jeans	GBR	1:16.0	IV	1:16.6 II		1:15.4
5 Iris Tanner	GBR	1:22.4	I	1:18.6 I		1:20.8
Gwitha Shand	NZL	1:21.0	IV	1:22.4 II		
Florence Barker	GBR	1:20.8	II	1:21.0 ii		
Marie Vierdag	NED	1:22.0	IV	1:21.2 I		
Mariette Protin	FRA	1:22.2	III	1:22.8 ii		
Hedevig Rasmussen	DEN	1:22.4	III			
Agnete Olsen	DEN	1:23.0	I			
Gulli Everlund	SWE	1:23.2	III			
Ernestine Lebrun	FRA	1:23.4	II			
Hjoris Topel	SWE	1:25.8	IV			
Vivan Pettersson	SWE	1:27.4	II			
Karen Rasmussen	DEN	1:29.0	II			

Women's 400 Meter Freestyle:		Trial		Semi		Final
1) Martha Norelius	USA	6:23.2	II	6:26.6	II	o6:02.2
2) Helen Waniwright	USA	6:46.8	III	6:19.6	I	6:03.8
3) Gertrude Ederle	USA	o6:12.2	I	6:23.8	II	6:04.8
4 Doris Molesworth	GBR	6:28.8	I	6:19.8	I	6:25.4
5 Gwitha Shand	NZL	6:26.6	IV	6:24.4	I	DNF
Iris Tanner	GBR	6:35.4	IV	6:34.0	II	
Connie Jeans	GBR	6:34.6	II	6:37.8	I	
Hedevig Rasmussen	DEN	6:58.2	I	6:55.2	II	
Mariette Protin	FRA	6:58,2	III	6:56.6	I	
Hjoris Topel	SWE	6:59.8	IV			
Vibeke Moller	DEN	7:02.2	III			
Maria Vierdag	NED	7:02.4	IV			
Gulli Everlund	SWE	7:05.4	I			
Ernestine Lebrun	FRA	7:06.4	I			
Geertriuda Klapwyk	NED	7:15.0	II			
Gilberthe Mortier	FRA	7:33.0	II			
Jane Gylling	SWE	7:55.0	III			
Ewe Chaloupkova	CZE	8:14.0	III			

Women's 100 Meter Backstroke:		Trial		Final
1) Sybil Bauer	USA	Lo1:24.0	I	Lo1:23.2
2) Phyllis Harding	GBR	1:29.6	I	1:27.4
3) Aileen Riggin	USA	1:29.6	II	1:28.2
4 Florence Chambers	USA	1:32.0	I	1:30.8
5 Jarmila Mullerova	TCH	1:37.0	II	1:31.2
Ellen King	GBR	1:38.2	I	
Helen Boyle	GBR	1:43.0	II	
Lucienne Rouet	FRA	1:43.8	I	
Alice Stoffel	FRA	1:44.0	II	
Renee Brasseur	LUX	1:51.4	II	

Women's 200 Meter Breaststroke:		Trial		Final
1) Lucy Morton	GBR	3:29.4	II	3:33.2
2) Agnes Geraghty	USA	Lo3:27.6	I	3:34.0
3) Gladys Carson	GBR	3:30.0	III	3:35.4
4 Vivan Pettersson	SWE	3:37.0	I	3:37.6
5 Irene Gilbert	GBR	3:32.8	I	3:38.0
6 Laury Koster	LUX	3:35.0	II	3:39.2
7 Hjordis Topel	SWE	3:39.0	III	3:47.6
Eleanor Coleman	USA	3:39.2	II	
Ella Molnar	HUN	3:39.8	II	
B. Drazkova	CZE	3:43.0	III	
Suzanne Kiffer Porte	FRA	3:43.6	III	
Alice Stoffel	FRA	3:48.0	II	
Odette Monard	FRA	3:48.4	I	
Marie Baron	NED	DQ3:22.6	I	

Women's 4x100 Meter Freestyle Relay: Final
1) USA (Ederle,Donnelly,Lackie,Wehselau) Lo4:58.8
2) GBR (Barker,Jeans,MacKenzie,Tanner) 5:17.0
3) SWE (Berg,Everlund,Petterson,Topel) 5:35.6
4 DEN (Moller,Olsen,H.Rasmussen,KM Rasmussen) 5:42.4
5 FRA (Lebrun Mortier,Pellegry,Protin) 5:43.4
6 NED (Baron,Bolten,Klapwijk,Vierdag) 5:45.8

1924 Women's Olympic Swimming Medals			1912-1924 Women's Olympic Swimming Medals		
	Gold	Medals		Gold	Medals
USA	4	10	USA	7	17
GBR	1	4	GBR	2	7
SWE	0	1	AUS	1	2
			SWE	0	2
			GER	0	1
			AUT	0	1

1928: Amsterdam, The Netherlands
(50-meter Outdoor, Fresh Water Pool)

Amsterdam Olympic pool (1928)

For the fifth straight Olympiad, the Games were held in Western Europe, with the swimming events in a cold, unheated outdoor pool. This not only worked against the warm-climate swimmers, but made it difficult to break existing records. However, the good Dutch organization and enthusiastic spectators did much to overcome this disadvantage.

The great meets of 1927 – the USA Outdoor Nationals in Honolulu, European Championships in Bologna and the Japan vs. USA Dual Meet in Tokyo — clearly indicated that Amsterdam 1928 would bring men's Olympic swimming to a new level. Going into the Games, four swimmers had already gone under a minute in the 100 free. Three men had cracked five minutes for the 400-meter free, six had dipped under three minutes in the 200 breast and four teams had bettered the Olympic record in the relay.

The most outstanding pre-Olympic performances were Johnny Weissmuller's "Big Pool" world best-ever times swum in Honolulu's salt-water, 110-yard War Memorial Pool: 58.0 for 100 meters, 2:13.6 for the 200, 4:52.0 for the 400 and 10:22.2 for the 800. Nearly as impressive were Arne Borg's times of 4:56.0, 10:09.0 and 19:07.2 for the 400, 800 and 1500 meters freestyle, swum at Bologna. The latter two were world records. Meanwhile, Andrew "Boy" Charlton – no longer a boy – had cut nearly seven seconds from his own Australian best in the 440 yard free with a 4:59.8 and over three seconds from his 1924 Australian record for 880 yards with a fast 10:32.0 at the New South Wales Championship meet in early 1927.

Men's 100 Meter Freestyle: The Olympic 100 meter freestyle field looked very deep with defending champion Johnny Weissmuller (USA) given only a slight edge. A year earlier, at the USA NAAU Meet in Honolulu, he had barely beaten schoolboy George Kojac from New York and Katsuo Takaishi from Japan. Their fast times of 58.0, 58.0 and 58.6 reflected the closeness of the race. Later in the season, Arne Borg (SWE), known for his distance prowess, swam 1:00.0 at the European Championships in Bologna while Walter Laufer (USA) clocked a 59.6 at the USA vs. Japan dual meet in Tokyo. Istvan Barany (HUN), from Eger, also kept himself in the Olympic medal picture by repeating as the 100–meter freestyle champion at the Hungarian Nationals with a fast 1:00.0 effort. Thus, the entries for Amsterdam included six men in the 100-meter free with times of one minute or better.

Johnny Weissmuller

But Weissmuller had a rendezvous with destiny, as he proved himself to be the world's fastest man by repeating as the Olympic 100 meter freestyle champion. Leading the strongest field ever through all three rounds with times of 1:00.0, 58.6 and 58.6, he left no doubt as to who was Number One. So dominant was Weissmuller that no other competitor came within a second of him in any round. In the final, Barany, the 1926 European champion, led the American through the first 50 meters in 27.0 before falling prey to Weissmuller's closing sprint. The Hungarian's second place time of 59.8 just edged bronze medalist Takaishi (1:00.0) with Kojac fourth in 1:00.8.

Men's 400 Meter Freestyle: The big surprise in the 400 meter freestyle occurred at the USA Trials in Detroit, a month before the Games, where Weissmuller, the defending Olympic champion decided not to swim this event. A year earlier he had clearly established himself as the world's best with his 4:52.0 for 440 yards in a 110-yad pool — four seconds faster than anyone else up to that time. Two weeks before the USA Tryouts he had won the Outdoor National title in San Francisco in 4:58.6, three seconds faster than the winning time in Amsterdam. Why did he not try for another Olympic gold medal in this event? Almost certainly he would have won again. Perhaps it was because the program of events had changed and they would have required him to swim eight races over five days, with his main final coming in the last session.

With Weissmuller watching from the grandstands, the 400 meter freestyle became an extremely competitive, wide-open event. In the heats, Clarence "Buster" Crabbe (USA), a strongly-built 20 year-old from the Honolulu Central YMCA and Arne Borg (SWE) from SKK in Stockholm, led the way with times of 5:07.8 and 5:09.6, respectively.

Argentina's Alberto Zorilla was the first South American to win Olympic gold in swimming, when he came storming from behind in the final 50 meters to win the 400-meter freestyle over favorites "Boy" Charlton, Arne Borg and Buster Crabbe.

The first semifinal featured a major upset as Argentina's Alberto Zorilla, who trained at the New York AC, upset Charlton (AUS) 5:11.4 to 5:13.6. In the second, Borg just outlasted Crabbe and the diminutive Austin Clapp (USA) from Hollywood AC, 5:05.6, to 5:06.2 and 5:06.8, respectively.

In the final, Borg sprinted to the front with a 1:02 first 100 meters and maintained that lead through the three-quarters mark. But his challengers were just biding their time. Over the final 100 meters, Zorilla, Charlton and Crabbe closed rapidly on the faltering Swede with the Argentine and the Aussie passing him close to the finish. Zorilla was the surprise victor in 5:01.6, with Charlton second in 5:03.6. Borg just managed to hold off Crabbe's late charge, 5:04.6 to 5:05.4, to gain the bronze medal.

Men's 1500 Meter Freestyle: The men's 1500 matched Arne Borg, the world record-holder and European champion, vs. Andrew "Boy" Charlton, the defending Olympic champion, and Buster Crabbe, the rising young star. By coincidence, these three were thrown together in the fifth and final preliminary heat. Borg won in 20:11.2, followed by Charlton (20:14.2) and Crabbe (20:17.2) - with

Albiuna Osipowich edged her American teammate, Eleanor Garatti, to win the 100-meter freestyle in an Olympic record 1:11.0.

The final turned out to be three races in one. In the struggle for the gold medal, Osipowich just beat Garatti, 1:11.0 to 1:11.4. The two British women were in a very close battle for third, with Cooper only a touch ahead of McDowall 1:13.6 to 1:13.8. Both were well under Cooper's British record of 1:14.8 from 1927 at Bologna. Laird defeated Lehmann for fifth 1:14.6 to 1:15.2. The Olympic mark of 1:12.2, set by Mariechen Wehselau in 1924 was eclipsed three times in Amsterdam: by Garatti in the semi and by Osipowich and Garatti in the final.

Women's 400 Meter Freestyle: Martha Norelius (USA) of New York's Women's Swimming Association (WSA) was favored to repeat as Olympic champion in the 400 meter freestyle. Since her 1924 triumph, she had improved greatly while winning eight U.S. freestyle titles and setting 11 world records. Other strong medal candidates included Marie Braun (NED) and Americans Ethel McGary and Josephine McKim.

In case any of her competitors had forgotten, Norelius wasted no time in establishing her ownership of the metric quarter mile. Tall and strong, she opened by breaking her own Olympic and world marks in the first preliminary with a 5:45.2. McGary, her WSA teammate, followed by taking the second heat in 6:04.2. McKim from the Carnegie Library SC won the third in 6:10.0 while Braun, from the ODZ club, swam away with the fourth in 5:53.8.

In the first semi, Norelius swam easily to win in 5:58.0 with Frederica Van der Goes from South Africa and Cissy Stewart (GBR) from Dundee, Scotland, well in arrears at 6:01.6 and 6:06.4. The second semi was a close, fast race between Braun and McKim, with the Dutch swimmer gaining the touch in 5:54.6 to 5:55.0 for McKim.

In the final, Norelius produced her greatest swim ever as she raced eight lengths of the Amsterdam pool in a world and Olympic record time of 5:42.8. Braun finished 15 seconds behind in 5:57.8, while McKim's 6:00.2 earned the bronze. . Well behind, Stewart, Van der Goes and Tanner trailed wih times of 6:07.0, 6:07.2 and 6:11.6.

Martha Norelius, another ace from the Women's Swimming Association (WSA) of New York, won the 400-meter freestyle by a full 15 seconds and set a world record of 5:42.8 in the process.

Women's 100 Meter Backstroke: With the absence of the 1924 champion, Sybil Bauer of the United Sates, and the 1927 European champion, Willie van den Turk from Holland, there was no clear pre-Olympic favorite in the 100 meter backstroke.

In the first of the three preliminary heats, Ellen King (GBR) from Zenith SC of Edinburgh finished in 1:22.0 to equal van den Turk's 1927 world record, setting an Olympic mark in the process. Marion Gilman (USA) from Neptune Beach SC was second in 1:24.0. Then, in the very next heat, Marie Braun (NED) from ODZ dropped the world standard to 1:21.6, as she was followed by American Lisa Lindstrom from the WSA in 1:23.0. The final prelim went to petite 14 year-old Eleanor Holm (USA), also from the WSA, who touched in 1:23.6, half a meter in front of Britain's Joyce Cooper at 1:24.2.

In the final, Cooper led for the first length only to be passed by Braun and King in an extremely close finish with Braun at 1:22.0, King 1:22.2 and Cooper 1:22.4. Three meters back the American trio stroked into the wall seemingly locked together, with Gilman fourth in 1:24.2, Holm fifth in the same time and Lindstrom sixth in 1:24.4.

Women's 200 Meter Breaststroke:

Based on the their performances in 1927 Else Jacobsen (DEN) from the DKG Club, Hilda Schrader (GER) from the Magdeburger DSV, Lotte Muhe (GER) of Hildesheim '99 and Mietje Baron (NED) from ODZ were considered the favorites for the Olympic breaststroke medals of 1928. The young Danish champion had swum 3:16.6 in Oslo, while the other three had turned in their best times of 3:19.4, 3:22.4 and 3:19.6, respectively, in the prelims of the European Championships in Bologna one year earlier.

At the German nationals in July, a month before the Amsterdam Games, Muhe set a world record in the Berlin 50-meter pool with a stunning 3:11.2, while Schrader was a strong second in 3:14.4.

Schrader threw down the gauntlet in the first heat, slashing Agnes Geraghty's Olympic record from 1924 by an astounding 16 seconds with her 3:11.6 – more than seven seconds ahead of second place Geraghty, whose 3:18.8 was by far her best ever. In the second of the preliminary heats, Muhe crushed Baron 3:14.2 to 3:20.2. Heat three went to Jacobsen, who dispatched the third German, Elfriede Zimmermann from G.W. Berlin, 3:17.6 to 3:18.6.

Hilde Schrader (GER) was the class of the women's 200-meter breaststroke field, slashing the Olympic record by 16 seconds in 3:11.2, before gliding to victory in 3:12.6.

In the first of the two semifinals, Baron reversed the decision on Muhe by winning in 3:15.4, with the German edging Jacobsen for second 3:16.8 to 3:17.4.

Schrader captured the other semi by more than ten seconds in 3:11.2, lowering her own, newly-minted Olympic record in the process. The time also equaled Muhe's long course world best, swum at the German championships earlier in the year.

Schrader won the gold with a time of only 3:12.6 – slower than her times in the first two rounds. Her swim suit had partially opened on the dive, slowing her throughout the race and putting her well behind the field at the start.

Jacobsen led through the first 100 in 1:29.8 before Schrader was able to come to the fore to finish well in front of her competition. In their third head-to-head race of these Games, Baron took the silver medal over Muhe with 3:15.4 to 3:16.8, just ahead of Jacobsen's 3:17.4.

Women's 4 x 100 Meter Freestyle Relay: With its host of top
100-meter freestylers, it was evident that, barring mishap, the USA should win the relay race in a breeze. However, a close, fiercely-fought race was anticipated for the other medals, with Britain, Germany and Holland likely in the fray.

After the USA's Lambert, Josephine McKim, Susan Laird and Albina Osipowich won the first heat of the 4x100 meter relay 4:55.6 – an Olympic record and world long course best time — it was clear that this event would not be closely contested since no other country had the potential to better five minutes.

In the final, the American team of Lambert, Eleanor Garatti, Osipowich and Norelius won as it pleased in the record time of 4:47.6, with Britain second in 5:02.8. South Africa took third over Germany, 5:13.4 to 5:14.4. Unfortunately, Holland, after swimming 5:04.0 for an apparent bronze medal, was disqualified on a relay exchange.

The USA women's 4 x 100m freestyle relay won as it pleased with a world best long course time of 4:47.6. No other country cracked five minutes. In white robes from left: Garatti, Lambert, Osipowich and Norelius.

Women's 400 Meter Freestyle

		Trial		Semi		Final
1) Martha Norilius	USA	Lo5:45.2	I	5:58.0	I	Wo5:42.8
2) Marie Braun	NED	5:53.8	IV	5:54.6	II	5:57.8
3) Josephine McKim	USA	6:10.0	III	5:55.0	II	6:00.2
4 Sarah "Cissie" Stewart	GBR	6:12.2	I	6:06.4	I	6:07.0
5 Frederica Van der Goes	SAF	6:03.6	IV	6:01.6	I	6:07.2
6 Vera Tanner	GBR	6:09.7	II	6:09.0	II	6:11.6
Ethel McGary	USA	6:04.2	II	No Time I		
Edith Mayne	GBR	6:10.8	IV	No Time II		
NK Miller	NZL	6:16.8	III	No Time I		
Vera Tanner	GBR	6:11.0	II			
Edna Davey	AUS	6:12.0	II			
Fritzi Lowy	AUT	6:20.1	III			
Trude Baumeister	NED	6:26.2	I			
Lotte Lehmannn	GER	6:28.0	II			
Dorie Schonemann	GER	6:37.0	I			
MM Ledoux	FRA	No Time I				
ME Bedford	SAF	No Time I				
D. Schoenemann	GER	No Time I				
R. Rennie	SAF	No Time II				
GP Roty	FRA	No Time II				
DV Lindberg	FIN	No Time III				
Reni Erkens	GER	No Time IV				

Women's 100 Meter Backstroke:

		Trial		Final
1) Marie Braun	NED	Wo1:21.6	II	1:22.0
2) Ellen King	GBR	Lo1:22.0	I	1:22.2
3) Joyce Cooper	GBR	1:24.2	III	1:22.8
4 Marion Gilman	USA	1:24.0	I	1:24.2
5 Eleanor Holm	USA	1:23.6	III	1:24.2
6 Lisa Lindstrom	USA	1:23.0	II	1:24.4
7 Elizabeth Stockley	NZL	1:25.4	I	1:25.8
Jeanne Grendel	NED	1:26.2	III	
Phyllis Harding	GBR	1:27.8	II	
Bonnie Mealing	AUS	No Time II		
Else Jacobsen	DEN	No Time III		
MJ Bernard	LUX	No Time III		

Women's 200 Meter Breaststroke:

		Trial		Semi		Final
1) Hilde Schrader	GER	o3:11.6	I	Lo3:11.2	II	3:12.6
2) Marie Baron	NED	3:20.2	II	3:15.4	I	3:15.2
3) Lotte Muhe	GER	3:14.2	II	3:16.8	I	3:17.6
4 Else Jacobsen	DEN	3:17.6	III	3:17.2	I	3:19.0
5 Margaret Hoffman	USA	3:21.6	II	3:22.4	II	3:19.2
6 Brita Hazelius	SWE	3:21.6	I	3:21.4	II	3:20.8
Elfriede Zimmermann	GER	3:18.6	III	No Time I		
Agnes Geraghty	USA	3:18.8	I	No Time I		
Marianne Gustavson	SWE	3:27.0	III	No Time I		
Van Norden	NED	3:27.2	IV	No Time II		
Jane Faunce	USA	3:29.0	IV	No Time II		

DM Thompson	AUS	3:33.6	IV	No Time	II
Margery Hinton	GBR	No Time	I		
C. van Gelder	NED	No Time	I		
Hedi Bienenfeld	AUT	No Time	II		
Mabel Hamblen	GBR	No Time	III		
D. Prior	CAN	No Time	III		
V. Rausch	LUX	No Time	II		
DE Gibbs	GBR	No Time	II		
R. Kaiserowna	POL	No Time	I		
Alice Stoffel	FRA	No Time	IV		

Women's 4x100 Meter Freestyle Relay:	Trial		Final
1) USA (Lambert,Osipowich,Garatti,Norelius)	Lo4:55.6	I	Lo4:47.6
2) GBR (Cooper,Stewart,Tanner,King)	5:16.6	II	5:02.8
3) SAF (Russell,Rennie,Bedford,van der Goes)	5:17.6	I	5:13.4
4 GER (Lehmann,Wunder,Schneider,Erkens)	5:19.0	II	5:14.4
5 FRA (Pellegry,Ledoux,Dupire,Horrent)	5:42.4	II	5:22.4
D NED (Smits,Baumeister,Vierdag,Braun)	5:08.8	I	DQ
DEN	No Time	I	

1928 Women's Olympic Swimming Medals

	Gold	Medals
USA	3	5
NED	1	3
GER	1	2
GBR	0	4
SAF	0	1

1912-1928 Women's Olympic Swimming Medals

	Gold	Medals
USA	10	22
GBR	2	11
GER	1	3
NED	1	3
AUS	1	2
SWE	0	2
SAF	0	1

1932: Los Angeles, USA
(Outdoor 50 Meter Pool)

L.A Olympic pool

After 28 years, the Olympic Games returned to America. The chosen city, Los Angeles, constructed superb facilities and produced a fine program. The L.A. Swim Stadium, built for these Olympics, featured a very fast, deep main pool, a warm-up pool and a stadium with seating for 10,000 spectators.

Since its first Olympics in 1920, Japan had made incredible progress in men's swimming. This Pacific Ocean island kingdom off the coast of China made its Olympic debut in 1920 with two swimmers who were unable to reach a final at the Antwerp Games. Four years later, Japan had finalists in four events, including Katsuo Takaishi with a fifth in both the 100- and 1500-meter freestyle; Takahiro Saito with a sixth in the 100 meter backstroke; and a 4x200 meter freestyle relay team that placed fourth. Then, in 1928 in Amsterdam, Japan earned its first Olympic medals: Yoshiyuki Tsuruta won the 200 meter breaststroke, Takaishi was third in the 100 meter freestyle and Japan was second in the 4x200 meter freestyle relay behind the USA.

Between 1928 and 1932, Japan continued to improve rapidly. By 1931, its men were first in the world in every Olympic event except the 100 meter backstroke. That same year, the Japanese men beat the Americans, 43-28, in a match in Tokyo, in which all the recognized metric events were contested. A year later, the Japanese team arrived in Los Angeles, fit, confident and eager to display its awesome talent on the world stage.

1932 MEN'S EVENTS

Men's 100 Meter Freestyle: Despite his youth, sixteen year-old Yasuji Miyazaki (JPN) was the leading contender for the gold medal in the 100 free. Swimming at the Japanese nationals a year earlier, the 15 year-old phenom had posted a 59.2, the fastest long course time in the world that year The only other swimmer to dip under a minute in a major long course meet in 1931 was Hungary's Istvan Barany, the veteran European champion, who clocked a 59.8. But Miyazaki issued his challenge to the world at the Japanese Tryouts in June of the Olympic year, qualifying first in 58.8.

There was no stopping the amazing Miyazaki in Los Angeles, as he led six men under the one-minute mark in the prelims of the 100 meter freestyle with a 58.7. Eight men bettered the one-minute barrier in the semifinals, with Miyazaki setting an Olympic record of 58.0— well under Johnny Weissmuller's 1928 mark of 58.6.

The final was made up of three Japanese and three Americans. The youthful Miyazaki was relentless as he stroked to a gold medal in 58.2, followed by Tatsugo Kawaishi (JPN) in 58.6 and Albert Schwartz (USA), from Northwestern University, in 58.8. Manuella Kalili (USA) from Los Angeles AC (59.2), Zenjiro Takahashi (JPN) (59.2) and Ray Thompson (USA) from the US Navy (59.5) finished fourth, fifth and sixth.

Fifteen year-old Yasuji Miyazaki (left) won the 100-meter freestyle in 58.2 seconds as teammate Tatsugo Kawaishi (right) gave Japan a one-two sweep. The USA's Albert Schwartz was third.

The final went to the more experienced Tsuruta after he waged a successful, all-out, two man battle with Koike, 2:45.4 to 2:46.6. Just as he had four yeas earlier, Sietas again lost the bronze medal to Yldefonzo, 2:47.1 to 2:48.0.

Men's 4 x 200 Meter Freestyle Relay: Perhaps the greatest of all the Japanese swimming victories in 1932 came in the relay. Beginning in 1920, this event had been the USA' private property. In the previous three Games, the Americans had not even been threatened by another country. As recently as 1931, the U.S. had beaten Japan by 17 seconds in their dual meet in Tokyo. However, after adding up each country's four best 200-meter times, only one second separated the two powerhouse countries. Most expected a very close contest in Los Angeles. However this did not happen.

After a brilliant leadoff of 2:14.0 by Japan's Miyazaki over Frank Booth's 2:20.2, Masanori Yusa, Takashi Yokoyama and Hisakichi Toyoda followed to give Japan the gold medal in the breath-taking time of 8:58.4 — nearly 38 seconds under the USA's Olympic record of 9:36.2 set just four years earlier. Although a badly beaten runner-up at 9:10.5, the USA team of Frank Booth, George Fissler (New York AC) and the Kalili brothers – Manuella and Marolo — from the Los Angeles AC, was 10 seconds faster than any previous American performance and was more than 20 seconds ahead of third place Hungary, whose 9:31.4, was a European record.

How did the Japanese swimmers accomplish their swimming miracle, going from nothing in 1920 to total control of men's Olympic swimming—and doing so on the USA's home turf — in 1932. So complete was their dominance that they outscored the rest of the world combined, 5-1 in gold medals and 11-7 in total medals.

To the surprise of no one, the 4 x 200-meter freestyle relay fell to the men of the Rising Sun. Their 8:58.4 – more than 12 seconds ahead of the second-place Americans – was a world record. From left: Miyazaki, Yusa, Toyoda, and Yokoyama.

Their amazing success was due to several factors that were part of Japanese culture: respect and love for the Emperor and their nation. Sport was one of the areas in which they could manifest these powerful emotions. When this strong feeling was combined with excellent organization and great discipline, impressive results could be expected to follow.

In the 1920's Japanese sporting leaders established strong club, high school and university swimming programs throughout the country. They developed excellent coaches at all levels to attract and prepare Japanese youth for success in this sport. The government built fine outdoor, 50-meter pools for the clubs, schools and universities. The emphasis was placed on summer outdoor training and competition in contrast to the United States, where high school and university swimming was – and still remains — mostly a short course winter sport.

1932 WOMEN'S EVENTS

Helene Madison of Seattle won three gold medals in Los Angeles – all in world record time – sparking the U.S. women to four wins in five events.

In contrast with the men, the American women in Los Angeles continued their winning ways of the 1920's. With three gold medals, Helene Madison of the Washington AC led the U.S. team to four wins in five events. Only the breaststroke eluded the Americans' quest for an Olympic sweep.

For the previous two-and-a-half years, the astonishing Madison had dominated American and world freestyle swimming completely. This very tall Seattle teenager had captured all 17 NAAU freestyle titles in the two previous outdoor and three previous indoor seasons. In a 16-month period, she set 21 world records from the 100 yard distance to the mile.

The three medalists in the women's 100 free. From left to right: Helene Madison, USA, first; Willi den Ouden, NED, second; and Eleanor Garatti-Seville, USA, third.

Women's 100 Meter Freestyle: Even though Helene Madison was favored because of her world record of 1:06.6, her world best long course performance of 1:08.2 and her numerous conclusive victories over her domestic rivals, there was still strong competition for this gold medal. The most dangerous were Eleanor Garatti-Saville, the silver medalist from 1928; Yvonne Godard (FRA), the European champion in 1:10.0 a year earlier; and Willi den Ouden (NED), who was second at the '31 European Championships in 1:11.8,

Strong competition began in the heats, in which five women swam more than one-and-a-half seconds under the Olympic record of 1:11.0. The fast swimming began in the second heat, with Joyce Cooper (GBR) from Mermaid SC of London outtouching Josephine McKim (USA) from the Los Angeles AC, 1:09.0 to 1:09.3.

In the next heat, Madison dropped the Olympic standard to 1:08.9 in an easy win over Jennie Maakal (SAF), who equaled the old mark of 1:11.0. Then Garatti-Saville (USA) from San Rafael, California lowered the mark even further with a 1:08.5 over 14-year-old den Ouden (NED) from the RDZ Club, who finished in 1:09.2.

In the first semifinal, the young Dutch girl swam away from Garatti-Saville, McKim and Cooper in Olympic and European record time of 1:07.6. She was far ahead of her rivals, who finished with times of 1:08.8, 1:08.8 and 1:09.2, respectively. An excited Madison overswam the first 50 in the second semi , fading badly at the end but hanging on to win her heat in a modest 1:09.9, ahead of Neville Bult (AUS) in 1:10.2 and Maakal (SAF) in 1:10.6.

In the final, a controlled first half produced a gold medal, an Olympic record and a world long course best time for Madison. Her new standard of 1:06.8 was just a second faster than den Ouden (1:07.8).. Veteran Garatti-Saville was a close third in 1:08.2. McKim (1:09.3) beat Bult (1:09.9) and Makaal (1:10.8) for fourth.

Helene Madison (left), with world record of 5:28.5, one-tenth of a second ahead of Lenore Kight (center), with Jennie Makaal South Africa third.

Women's 400 Meter Freestyle: To win the gold medal in the 400 meter freestyle, Helene Madison knew she would have to turn back a very strong challenge from fellow American Lenore Kight from the Carnegie Library AC in Pittsburgh. Kight had finished second behind Madison five times in the middle distance events at the 1931 U.S. National Championships. From Europe, there were three strong contenders for medals:Marie Braun Philipsen (NED), Joyce Cooper (GBR) and Yvonne Godard (FRA). They were the first three at the 1931 European Championships in Paris with times of 5:42.0, 5:54.0 and 5:55.4, respectively.

Madison beat Braun-Philipsen from the ODZ Club in the second heat, 5:44.5 to 5:50.5. In the next heat, Kight broke the Olympic record from 1928 by two seconds with a fine 5:40.9, placing her nearly 10 ten seconds ahead of "Puck" Oversloot (NED). In the semis, both of the Americans eased off, with Madison taking the first in 5:48.7 and Kight the second in 5:50.8 as the rest of the field finished far behind in both races.

As expected, the final quickly developed into a battle royal between these two great swimmers. They swam together through the first 200 meters in 2:38 — faster than the world long course best for that distance. Over the third 100, Madison carved a tiny lead for herself which, despite Kight's repeated challenges, she held to the finish. Her time of 5:28.5 was a world and Olympic record, four seconds under her own previous world long course best from the USA Tryouts a month earlier. Kight finished a mere tenth of a second behind in 5:28.6. South Aftican Jennie Maakal was a distant third (5:47.3), a body length in front of Cooper (5:49.7).

Women's 100 Meter Backstroke:

Even though the 100 meter backstroke had only 12 entries, the quality performers were all there. The field featured the last four world record-holders: Marie Braun-Philipsen (NED), Bonnie Mealing (AUS), Phyllis Harding (GBR) and Eleanor Holm (USA). This group included the defending Olympic champion, the European champion, and the British Empire champion. This was easily the deepest field ever assembled to contest a women's backstroke race.

In the first heat, Holm from the WSA of New York, crushed Mealing, Harding and Oversloot (NED) with a 1:18.3 to 1:21.6, 1:22.5 and 1:23.5, respectively. Holm's time was only a tenth off her own world record of 1:18.2, set at the USA Tryouts a month earlier. Valerie Davies took the second heat in 1:22.5 and Braun-Philipsen won the third in 1:23.8.

Holm built a small lead over the first length of the final before sprinting home the last 25 meters to win easily in 1:19.4. Mealing was a distant second in 1:21.3, followed by the two Englishwomen, Davies and Harding, in 1:22.5 and 1:22.6.

Eleanor Holm (USA), the world record-holder, cruised to victory in the 100-meter backstroke.

Australia's Claire Dennis won a very tight 200-meter breaststroke race in a world record 3:06.3.

Women's 200 Meter Breaststroke: With all three of the 1928 medalists retired, the 200 meter breaststroke figured to be a struggle among several young swimmers who were on the way up. Prominent among them were Celia Wolstenholme (GBR) from the Moss Side SC, the Empire Games and European champion; Claire Dennis (AUS), the former world record-holder; Hideko Maehata (JPN), the world's fastest long course swimmer in 1930 and 1931; and world record-holder Else Jacobsen (DEN) from the DKG Club.

In the first of three preliminary heats, Dennis swam 3:08.2, three seconds under the Olympic record and world long course best time (3:11.2) set by Lotte Muhe and Hilda Schrader of Germany in 1928. She finished six-and-a-half seconds in front of Margaret Hoffman (USA) from the Scranton SA. In the second heat, Jacobsen easily swam away from Anne Govednik (USA) from Minnesota, 3:12.1 to 3:15.9. Wolstenholme (GBR), a distant third, did not qualify for the final. Maehata took the third heat in 3:10.7, ahead of Margery Hinton (GBR) from Old Trafford (3:13.5).

The hotly contested final quickly became a three woman battle among Dennis,

Maehata and Jacobsen. For 175 meters, the 16-year-old Dennis held a tiny lead over Jacobsen. Then, in the last half length of the race, the young Dane fell off the pace, allowing Maehata to pass her and finish within inches of Dennis. Their medal-wining times of 3:06.3, 3:06.4 and 3:07.1 were far faster than Dennis' world long course best time from the heats.

Women's 4 x100 Meter Freestyle Relay: In keeping with their tradition of the three previous Olympic Games, the USA freestyle relay team easily won the 4x100 meter event by nearly 10 seconds, in world and Olympic record time. The quartet of Josephine McKim, Helen Johns, Eleanor Garatti-Saville and Helene Madison dropped the world and Olympic marks from 4:47.6 to 4:38.0. Also under the old standards was second place Holland (4:47.5), which finished ahead of Britain (4:52.4).

The USA's 4 x 100-meter freestyle relay was unchallenged in setting a world record of 4:38.0. From left: McKim, Johns, Garatti-Saville and Madison.

1932 OLYMPIC SWIMMING RESULTS
LOS ANGELES, CALIFORNIA
OUTDOOR 50 METER POOL

Men's 100 Meter Freestyle:

		Trial		Semi		Final
1) Yasuji Miyazaki	JPN	58.7	IV	o58.0	I	58.2
2) Tatsugo Kawaishi	JPN	59.8	II	59.0	II	58.6
3) Albert Schwartz	USA	59.6	II	59.2	II	58.8
4 Manuella Kalili	USA	59.6	I	59.3	I	59.2
5 Zenjiro Takahashi	JPN	59.5	III	59.5	II	59.2
6 Ray Thompson	USA	1:02.0	III	59.3	I	59.5
Istvan Barany	HUN	1:00.4	I	59.4	I	
Walter Spence	CAN	59.3	II	59.6	II	
Andrew Szekely	HUN	1:01.5	IV	1:01.4	I	
Munroe Bourne	CAN	1:01.1	I			
Abdurahman Ali	PHI	1:02.2	IV			
Andras Wanie	HUN	1:02.8	II			
Noel Ryan	AUS	1:02.9	IV			
Reg Sutton	GBR	1:02.9	I			
Alfredo Rocca	ARG	1:04.2	III			
Joseph Whiteside	GBR	1:04.7	III			
Leopold Tahier	ARG	1:05.3	I			
MY French-Williams	GBR	1:05.9	II			
Eskil Lundahl	SWE	1:06.2	III			
Robert Halloran	CAN	1:06.9	IV			
Manuel Villar	BRA	1:08.1	I			
Joao Pereira	BRA	1:08.2	III			

Men's 400 Meter Freestyle:

		Trial		Semi		Final
1) Clarence "Buster" Crabbe	USA	4:59.8	II	4:52.7	II	Lo4:48.4
2) Jean Taris	FRA	4:53.3	IV	4:52.3	I	4:48.5
3) Tsutomu Oyakota	JPN	5:06.3	V	4:52.8	I	4:52.3
4 Takashi Yokoyama	JPN	o4:53.2	I	Lo4:51.4	I	4:52.5
5 Noboru Sugimoto	JPN	5:00.2	II	4:59.0	II	4:58.6
6 Andrew "Boy" Charlton	AUS	4:59.8	III	5:02.1	II	4:58.6
Jim Gilhula	USA	4:53.3	I	4:55.4	I	
Noel Ryan	AUS	5:01.9	V	4:59.7	I	
Paolo Costoli	ITA	5:06.7	III	5:06.0	I	
Giuseppe Perentin	ITA	5:09.1	IV	5:10.5	II	
Walter Spence	CAN	5:10.0	III	5:15.6	II	
Norman Wainwright	GBR	5:12.0	II			
Bob Leivers	GBR	5:14.6	IV			
George Larson	CAN	5:20.1	V			
George Burrows	CAN	5:28.9	I			
Ignacio Escoto	MEX	5:29.1	II			
Juljus Kanassy	HUN	5:40.8	III			
Manuel Bouchez	MEX	5:54.2	III			
Nalin Malik	IND	5:59.0	IV			

1936: Berlin, Germany
(Outdoor 50 Meter Pool)

The Berlin City Pool, built for the 1936 Olympic Games.

In the four short years between Los Angeles and Berlin, a lot had happened to change the scene in the world of swimming. Three major meets had much to do with these rearrangements: the British Empire Games and the European Championships in August of 1934, and the Japan vs. USA dual meet for men in August of 1935. The U.S. women were the only strong team not included in these competitions. This may have been one of the reasons for their mediocre results in Berlin in 1936.

Each of the three meets highlighted changes in the strengths and weaknesses of both nations and individuals. The Empire Games in London clearly demonstrated how far Britain and her colonies had fallen behind in international swimming. Canada was the dominant nation in London, but its times were well below Olympic medal level. At the Europeans in Magdeburg, Germany was the leading country in the men's events, while Holland completely dominated the women's races, capturing four out of five titles. These Dutch winners were also the best in the world for

1934. In Tokyo, Japan again out-pointed the US men in 1935, but they were not quite as dominant as they had been in Los Angeles three years earlier. Even without their two best backstrokers, the Americans were competitive, losing by a score of 36-27 – a much closer score than the 40-23 defeat they had suffered in 1931. This improvement by the U.S. men was on display the next year in Berlin.

For the 1936 Games, Germany had constructed a fine outdoor swimming stadium with an eight-lane, 50-meter racing pool and a 20-meter-square diving facility. Surrounding the competition area were steeply angled stands with seating for 20,000 spectators as well as standing-room-only sections for another 5,000 people. Unfortunately, cool, rainy weather did much to slow the performances of many of the swimmers.

1936 MEN'S EVENTS

Men's 100 Meter Freestyle: Great performances were expected in this sprint contest. After all, for two years there had been a steady buildup in the hype for the 100 meters, featuring two Europeans, an American and three Japanese. At the 1934 European Championships, Ferenc Csik (HUN) from BEAC and Helmut Fischer (GER) from the Bremischer SV first revealed their Olympic potential by finishing first and second in 59.7 and 59.8. The next year, these two dropped their long course times to 57.8 and 58.4, respectively, to show the world they were ready for the Berlin Games in 1936.

In the USA, Peter Fick, a big, strong New Yorker, had become the top domestic 100-meter man in 1934 with a world record of 56.8 in a 25-meter course. In the Tokyo match with Japan the next year he won in a world long course best time of 57.2. Four weeks later, Masanori Yusa (JPN) from Nihon University tied this performance in the same pool at the Japanese University Championships.

In Berlin, the men's 100 meter freestyle started explosively as five men broke the 1932 Olympic record of 58.0 in the preliminaries: Peter Fick (USA), from the New York AC with a 57.7 in the first heat; Masanori Yusa (JPN) with a 57.8 in the second heat; Shigeo Arai (JPN) of Rikkyo University, and Helmut Fischer (GER) with 57.7 and 57.9, respectively, in the third heat; and Shoji Taguchi (JPN), Rikkyo University, with the fastest preliminary time, a 57.5, in the fifth heat.

In the first semifinal, Taguchi won in 57.9, ahead of Csik (58.1), Fick (58.2) and Fischer (58.7). Yusa matched Taguchi's Olympic mark from the heats with a 57.5 in the second semi, ahead of Arai (57.9) and Art Lindegren (USA) from the Los Angeles AC (58.7).

In one of the most controversial finals in Olympic history, Csik captured the gold medal (57.6), followed by Yusa (57.9) and Arai (58.0) for silver and bronze. Taguchi placed fourth (58.1) while fifth was awarded to Fischer (59.3) over Fick (59.7) and Lindegren (59.9). The cause of the questionable order of finish was the FINA judging system of that period, which required each finish judge to pick all of the finalists. Modern officials would consider such a system impossible to execute. Many officials, coaches and journalists felt that after Csik, the order of finish was questionable. Carl Wooten of Great Britain's *Swimming Times* wrote an article with a photo indicating that the order should have been: Csik, Fick, Taguchi, Yusa, Arai, Fischer and Lindegren.

Ferenc Csik of Hungary won the 100-meter freestyle in one of the most controversial races in Olympic history.

Men's 400 Meter Freestyle: Based on the USA-Japan competition in 1934 and 1935, the 400 meter freestyle figured to be a struggle between Jack Medica (USA) from the Washington AC and several Japanese swimmers. Although the bespectacled American had won both times he had faced the Japanese, his 1935 margin of victory at the Japan-USA match in Tokyo was less than one-tenth of a second over Hirosi Negami. Both men were clocked in 4:45.2, with the veteran Shozo Makino a close third in 4:46.8.

At the Japanese and the American tryouts before the 1936 Games, there were some changes on each team in the 400-meters. At Rocky Point, R.I., Ralph Flanagan from the Greater Miami AC upset the favored Medica in 4:47.8, with John Macionis (Yale University) third. In Tokyo, Shumpei Uto qualified in 4:54.4 ahead of Noboru Terada and Hirosi Negami. Later, Terada withdrew to concentrate on the 1500 and was replaced by Makino.

In the preliminaries, only Shumpei Uto showed his true form with a brilliant 4:45.5 — nearly three seconds under Buster Crabbe's 1932 Olympic record. The next two qualifiers for the semis were his teammates, Shozo Makino and Hirose Negami, at 4:51.5 and 4:52.6. The next round saw Uto beat Flanagan, with a 4:48.4

to the American's 4:54.9. The second semi produced a close battle with Makino out-touching Medica, although both men were clocked in 4:48.2.

The 400 meter final turned out to be the titanic struggle that had been expected. Uto led at the halfway point with a strong 2:19.9 — inches ahead of Medica and Negami. At 300 meters Uto extended his small advantage to more than two meters. Over the last 100, Medica caught and passed Uto to finish in an Olympic record 4:44.5 — the fastest long course time ever. Uto held off Makino for the silver medal, 4:45.6 to 4:48.1. Well behind the three medalists were Flanagan (4:52.7), Negami (4:53.6) and Jean Taris, the 1932 runner up from France (4:53.8).

The USA's Jack Medica snagged the 400-meter freestyle crown in an Olympic record 4:44.5. Japan's Shumpei Uto and Shozo Makino took the silver and bronze medals.

Men's 1500 Meter Freestyle

Men's 1500 Meter Freestyle: In 1935, seven of the world's 10 fastest men in the 1500 were Japanese. Their incredible work ethic had made this possible. Only Americans Jack Medica and Ralph Flanagan stood even a remote chance of preventing a Japanese sweep in Berlin. In the 1935 Japan vs. USA dual meet in Tokyo, held only a year before the Berlin Games, the Japanese had finished 1-2-3 in the 1500. Sunao Ishiharada (19:12.0), Shozo Makino (19:21.8) and Hirosi Negami (19:22.8) had left Medica (19:35.8) and Flanagan (19:52.6) floundering, far behind, in their wakes. As for the rest of the world, no other swimmer stood a realistic chance of bringing home a medal.

At the Games, five men bettered 20 minutes in the preliminaries: Medica, Flanagan and the three Japanese. In the first semifinal, Noboru Terada led Flanagan, 19:48.6 to 19:59.4 Medica, however, was the surprise winner of the second semi, posting the fastest qualifying time, 19:42.8, easily out-distancing Ishiharada and Uto from Japan and Heinz Arendt (GER) in 19:53.9, 19:55.6 and 19:56.1, respectively.

Noburu Terada extended Japanese dominance of the longest swimming race, winning the 1500 meters in 19:13.7, missing Kasuo Kitamura's Olympic record from Los Angeles by just over as second.

After passing through the 400 mark in the final in a fast 4:57, Terada drew steadily away from the others, splitting 10:07 at the 800 and reaching the finish in 19:13.7, just over Kitamura's 1932 Olympic mark. Medica sprinted to gain the silver medal over Uto, 19:34.0 to 19:34.5. The last four finishers all managed to break 20 minutes. Ishiharada outswam Flanagan for fourth with a 19:48.5 to 19:54.8, ahead of Robert Leivers (GBR) (19:57.4) and Arendt (19:59.0).

Men's 100 Meter Backstroke
Still smarting from the Japanese backstroke sweep at the Los Angeles Games four years earlier, the United States began to regain control of this Olympic event. In 1934, U.S. schoolboy Albert Vandeweghe won the Japanese national titles in both the 100 and 200 meter events by large margins over Kiichi Yoshida, clocking 1:08.8 and 2:33.2. The latter time was more than two seconds faster than Kiyokawa's world long course best from 1932. Competing in a meet in Honolulu during the summer of 1934, Vandeweghe dropped the short course 100-meter backstroke world record to 1:07.4.

In 1935, Adolph Kiefer — another U.S. schoolboy (Lake Shore AC), from Chicago — appeared suddenly on the national and international scene. On a tour of Germany, he lowered Vandeweghe's short course world record three times to 1:04.9. He also posted a long course world record of 1:05.6 in Coral Gables, Florida, at the end of the year — far below the previous mark of 1:08.2, set by George Kojac (USA) at the 1928 Games.

Adolph Kiefer (USA), the most dominant backstroker of all time, took the 100-meter backstroke crown in 1936 with an Olympic record 1:05.9.

The 100 meter backstroke was the best swimming event for the Americans in these politically-charged Games. With world record-holder Adolph Kiefer leading the way, the Americans were simply unbeatable. In the first heat, Kiefer bested defending champion Kiyokawa (JPN) with both men finishing well below George Kojac's record time of 1:08.2 set in 1928. Their times of 1:06.9 and 1:07.2, however, were still well behind Kiefer's 1935 long course standard of 1:05.6. No one else was able to better 1:09.0 in the heats.

In the first semifinal, Kiefer won convincingly over teammate Albert Vandeweghe, 1:06.8 to 1:08.6. Taylor Drysdale (USA) from the Detroit AC, beat Kiyokawa in the other semi, 1:08.6 to 1:09.7.

The final pitted three Japanese and an Australian against the three Americans.

Leading all the way, Kiefer smashed his own Olympic mark from the heats with a fine 1:05.9. Vandeweghe won the silver over Kiyokawa, 1:07.7 to 1:08.4,. Drysdale's 1:09.4 was good for fourth, ahead of Japan's Kiichi Yoshida (1:09.7).

Japan's Tetsuo Hamuro (right) beat Germany's Erwin Sietas in the 200-meter breaststroke, the third Olympiad in a row that the event was won by a Japanese swimmer.

Men's 200 Meter Breaststroke: Following the Los Angeles Games, silver medalist Reizo Koike (JPN) emerged as the world's best long course 200 meter breaststroker, a distinction he maintained for four years. Only Tetsuo Hamuro (JPN), Teofilo Yldefonzo from the Philippines and John Higgins (USA), from the Olneyville BC, had even approached his performances. However, the world record during this same four-year stretch had belonged to quite another group of athletes, mostly short course specialists: Jacques Cartonnet (FRA) from Paris, Erwin Sietas (GER) from Bremen and Jack Kasley (USA) from the University of Michigan.

In the first of five heats, Hamuro destroyed Koike's 1932 Olympic record of 2:44.9 with a 2:42.5. This second-fastest long course performance of all time was well ahead of Sietas (2:44.6), the veteran finalist from 1928 and 1932. The only other swimmer to dip under the 2:45 barrier was Koike in 2:43.8.

The first semifinal went to Koike in 2:44.5 to 2:45.4 for Joachim Balke (GER) from Dortmund and 2:45.5 for Saburo Ito (JPN). In the second semi, Hamuro beat Higgins, 2:43.4 to 2:44.0. Sietas was a close third in 2:44.8, well ahead of Yldefonzo (2:46.6). Both had been finalists in the 1928 and 1932 Games.

The final turned out to be a fine battle between Hamuro and Sietas, with the Japanese swimmer leading all the way to finish in 2:42.5, equaling his Olympic mark from the first heat. With a strong last length, Sietas just missed the gold medal, touching the wall in 2:42.9, half-a-meter behind his rival. Koike beat Higgins for the bronze medal, 2:44.2 to 2:45.2. Interestingly, Higgins and seventh place finisher Joachim Balke swam the new butterfly arm stroke for part of the distance in the final.

The Japanese had a surprisingly easy time winning the 4 x 200-meter freestyle relay, defeating arch-rival USA by 11.5 seconds. Leading the entire race, Japan posted a world record 8:51.5. From left: Sugiura, Arai, Yusa, and Taguchi.

Men's 4 x 200 Meter Freestyle Relay: Considering the results of the 1932 Games, the 1934 European Championships and the 1935 Japan vs. USA dual meet, the Japanese, Americans and Hungarians — in that order — were heavily favored to win the medals in the relay final. They had finished in that order in Los Angeles, posting times of 8:58.4, 9:10.5 and 9:31.1. In Magdeburg, Hungary had won the European title over Germany in 9:30.2; while Japan had defeated the U.S. in Tokyo the next year, 8:52.2 to 8:58.6, in their dual meet.

In the preliminaries of the relay, three teams shattered the European record of 9:28,8. In heat one, a surprising French squad clocked 9:21.7. That time stood as a continental standard only until the next heat, where Hungary's 9:20.8 just nipped Germany's 9:21.4. Then, in the third and final heat, Japan produced an Olympic record of 8:56.1.

In the final, Yusa (JPN) led off by grabbing a two-second lead over Flanagan

(USA) with a fast 2:13.4 Inexorably, Japan steadily increased its lead before winning the gold in the world record time of 8:51.5 — an impressive 11.5 seconds ahead of the USA. Finishing a strong third behind the Americans' 9:03.0 was Hungary in 9:12.3,, lowering its European mark from the heats.

Well behind the Hungarians, France outtouched Germany for fourth, 9:18.2 to 9:19.0. Britain was a close sixth in 9:21.5. Canada, which finished seventh in 9:27.5, was eight seconds faster than any winning Olympic relay team before 1932.

1936 WOMEN'S EVENTS

In the women's events, the big question was whether or not the isolated Americans could stand up against the new, high level of swimming in Europe after four Olympics of unparalleled success. Headed by the Dutch, the European women — greatly improved since Magdeburg — were formidable. From the USA team, only Lenore Kight-Wingard in the 400 meter free and veteran Eleanor Holm-Jarret in the backstroke appeared to have title chances. Unfortunately, the latter's expulsion from the American team on the way to Berlin further reduced the U.S. hopes.

Holland's Hendrika "Rie" Mastenbroek was the female star of the 1936 Games, with gold medals in the 100- and 400-meter freestyle and the 4 x 100-meter free relay.

Women's 100 Meter Freestyle: With six women at or under 1:08.0 for the long course 100, a tough, fast Olympic struggle was expected in Berlin. During 1932 – 1936, Willi den Ouden had lowered the world short course record from 1:06.0 to 1:04.6. Even more impressively, she had reduced Helene Madison's world long course best of 1:06.8 from 1932 to 1:05.2 in 1935. Her main continental rivals were powerful Hendricka "Rie" Mastenbroek (NED), Gisela Arendt (GER) and Renée Blondeau (FRA) with long course best times of 1:07.2, 1:06.7 and 1:08.0, respectively. From Argentina, tall Jeanette Campbell, the 1935 South American champion at 1:08.0, and Kitty McKay (AUS) with a 1:08.2 for 110 yards in Sydney, rounded out the list of main contenders. No American appeared to be in contention in this event.

The 100 meter freestyle began auspiciously for Holland as Mastenbroek, from the ODZ Club, finished the first heat well ahead of Arendt (GER) from Nixe Charlottenburg in an Olympic record time of 1:06.4 to 1:07.3 for the Berliner. World record-holder den Ouden won a close battle with Evelyn de Lacy (AUS) in the second heat, 1:08.1 to 1:08.5. The third Dutch entrant, Tini Wagner, was soundly beaten in the third heat by Argentina's Campbell, 1:06.8 to 1:08.9. In the last two heats no one bettered 1:09.0.

The first semifinal saw Mastenbroek continue her winning ways as she again outswam Arendt and broke the Olympic record with a 1:06.4 to a 1:07.2 for her German rival. Campbell outtouched den Ouden in the other semi with a fast 1:06.6 to 1:06.7.

The final, which was precisely the pitched battle knowledgeable spectators imagined it would be, featured Mastenbroek passing her three main rivals with a powerful finish over the last 25 meters. Her gold medal swim of 1:05.9, again an Olympic mark, placed her a scant meter in front of the pace-setting Campbell and Arendt. Their times of 1:06.4 and 1:06.6 put them well clear of the fading den Ouden (1:07.6). Wagner held off Americans Olive McKean and Katherine Rawls for fifth, with 1:08.1 to 1:08.4 and 1:08.7.

Women's 400 Meter Freestyle: Coming into the Games, the favorites for this event were Lenore Kight-Wingard (USA) second in 1932 with a 5:28.6; the Dutch duo of Willi den Ouden and Rie Mastenbroek, who had finished together at the 1934 European Championships in 5:27.4; and Ragnhild Hveger (DEN), who had swum 5:21.5 at the 1936 Danish nationals. Unfortunately, den Ouden, who held the short course world record of 5:16.0, gave up the 400 after 1934.

As in the 100 meter free, the 400 had an explosive start in the preliminaries. Fifteen year-old Hveger, from the HS Club, won the first heat in the Olympic record time of 5:28.0, well ahead of Kight-Wingard and the Brazilian champion, Azeveda Coutinho, who finished in 5:34.0 and 5:35.5. In the other heats, only Grete Frederiksen (DEN), from the DKG Club, and Mastenbroek dipped under 5:40, with times of 5:39.3 and 5:38.6, respectively.

The first semi saw Mastenbroek coast in ahead of Kight-Wingard and

Frederiksen in 5:40.3 to 5:42.2 and 5:42.5. Hveger made short work of her competition in the second semi as she swam away from Coutinho with an easy 5:33.7 to 5:42.3.

In the hard-fought final, the young Hveger led her powerful Dutch rival until the final 50 meters, where Mastenbroek's superior speed produced victory. Both women bettered Hveger's Olympic standard of 5:28.0 from the heats with times of 5:26.4 and 5:27.5. Kight-Wingard won the bronze medal over USA teammate Mary Lou Petty from the Washington AC, 5:29.0 to 5:32.2. Due to an error in timing, the third place time was unofficial.

Another Dutch swimmer, Dina "Nida" Senff, took the 100-meter backstroke despite completely botching her turn. Mastenbroek was second.

Women's 100 Meter Backstroke: In

the absence of American Eleanor Holm-Jarrett, the women's backstroke looked to be an all-European affair. In the very first heat, Dina Senff (NED), from the ADZ Club, astounded the swimming world with a winning time of 1:16.6. This performance was an Olympic record and a world long course best. At 1:20.4, Dane Tove Brunstroem, from the Triton Club, was a distant second. Alice Bridges (USA), from Massachusetts, took the second heat in 1:19.2. The third went to Edith Mottridge (USA) from the Los Angeles AC, ahead of Rie Mastenbroek, 1:21.0 to 1:22.0.

Senff easily swam off with the first semifinal with another fast time, 1:17.1, to finish with open water between herself and Mottridge, Brunstroem and Phyllis Harding (GBR), the 1924 silver medalist. Their times were 1:19.1, 1:19.7 and 1:19.8. Mastenbroek won the second semi in 1:19.0, one meter ahead of Lorna Frampton (GBR), 1:19.6.. Bridges was third another meter behind in 1:20.4.

In the final, Senff built a two-meter lead over the first length before she botched the turn, allowing six swimmers to pass her. From a dead start, she battled her way back into the lead again with 20 meters to go. After holding off the closing efforts of Mastenbroek and Bridges, she touched first in 1:18.9. The powerful Mastenbroek just beat Bridges ,1:19.2 to 1:19.4, for the silver medal with the other American, Mottridge, a close fourth in 1:19.6.

Japan's Hideko Maehata was golden in the 200-meter breaststroke, the only women's event in Berlin not won by the Dutch.

Women's 200 Meter Breaststroke:

Throughout 1934 and 1935, Hideko Maehata (JPN) and Martha Genenger (GER), from Neptun Krefeld Club, were the two leaders in women's breaststroke. As well as being the silver medal-winner from the 1932 Games, Maehata was the world record-holder at 3:00.4, swum in 1933 in a 25-meter pool. Genenger was the European winner in 1934 and German champion from 1934-1936.

The Berlin event started well when 12-year-old Inge Sorensen (DEN) from the DKG Club swam the first heat in 3:06.7, only a few tenths of a second above the Olympic record from 1932. Genenger won the next heat in 3:03.0, an Olympic mark and world long course best. The third heat went to Maehata in the even faster time of 3:01.9.

Maehata swam away from Sorensen in the first semifinal, 3:03.1 to 3:06.0. But Genenger threw down a challenge by winning the second semi by more than six seconds in 3:02.8. Jennie Kastein (NED) took the second place over Doris Storey (GBR), 3:09.2 to 3:09.8.

The final produced the anticipated struggle between the Japanese and German champions. Maehata led by less than a meter all the way to win in 3:03.6 to Genenger's 3:04.2.. Sorensen fought off the rest of the field to take the bronze medal in 3:07.8. Hanni Holzner, "Jopie" Waalberg (NED) and Storey nearly finished together in 3:09.5, 3:09.5 and 3:09.7 for the next three places.

Women's 4 x 100 Meter Freestyle Relay: Before the Berlin Games, the women's relay looked like a Dutch affair, as it was evident that the U.S. team was not what it had been in the 1920-32 period. No one had stepped up to replace Helene Madison or Eleanor Garatti-Saville. Indeed, with Gisela Arendt and others, Germany might even challenge the Americans for the silver medal.

After the preliminaries, in which Holland missed the Olympic record of 4:38.0 set by the USA in 1932 by only one tenth of a second, it looked as though the Dutch could cruise to victory in the final — especially with three of the world's top five 100-meter swimmers representing Holland. Germany, which swam in the same heat as Holland, turned in a national record of 4:40.5, while Denmark was third in 4:46.2. The USA won the first prelim over Britain and qualified fourth for the final in 4:47.1.

In the final, the USA led for the first two legs with Katharine Rawls, from the Miami Beach SC, and Bernice Lapp, from the Newark AC staying ahead of the Dutch and German teams. Then, den Ouden passed 14-year-old Ingrid Schmitz from the Spandau 04 Club, and Mavis Freeman from the WSA of New York to put Holland ahead. On the anchor, Arendt moved Germany in front on the first 50, only to fall before Mastenbroek's withering final sprint.

Holland won with an Olympic record and world long course best time of 4:36.0. Germany was a close second, only 8-tenths of a second in arrears. The Americans, who faded badly on the last two legs, could only muster a 4:40.2 for the bronze medal.

The Dutch 4 x 100-meter freestyle relay team, which pipped Germany by eight-tenths of a second for the gold, is escorted to the victory podium. From left: GER: Halbsguth, Lohmar, Schmitz, Arendt, NED: Selbach, Wagner, denOuden, Mastenbroek, and USA: Rawls, Lapp, Freeman, McKean.

1936 OLYMPIC SWIMMING RESULTS
BERLIN, GERMANY
OUTDOOR 50 METER POOL

Men's 100 Meter Freestyle:		Trial		Semi		Final
1) Ferenc Csik	HUN	58.3	I	58.1	I	57.6
2) Masanori Yusa	JPN	57.8	II	o57.5	II	57.9
3) Shigeo Arai	JPN	o57.7	IV	57.9	II	58.0
4 Shoji Taguchi	JPN	o57.5	V	57.9	I	58.1
5 Helmut Fischer	GER	57.9	IV	58.7	I	59.3
6 Peter Fick	USA	o57.7	I	58.2	I	59.7
7 Arthur"Art" Lindegren	USA	58.3	VII	58.7	II	59.9
Arthur"Art" Highland	USA	59.9	II	59.4	II	
Willy Kendall	AUS	1:01.0	II	59.9	II	
Hermann Heibel	GER	1:01.4	VI	1:00.3	II	
HJ Heitenen	FIN	1:01.0	VII	1:00.5	I	
MY French-Williams	GBR	1:00.7	III	1:01.0	I	
Oszkar Nemes	HUN	1:00.2	VII	1:01.1	II	
Wilfan	YUG	1:00.6	VI	1:00.5	I	
Jikirum Adjaluddin	PHI	1:01.0	III	1:00.5	I	
John Christensen	DEN	1:01.2	V	1:01.6	II	
R. Gabrielson	GBR	1:01.2	I			
Odon Grof	HUN	1:01.3	IV			
Piet Stam	NED	1:01.3	VII			
Hermann Heibel	GER	1:01.4	VI			
John Larson	CAN	1:01.5	V			
E. Roolaid	EST	1:01.5	II			
Paul Petersen	DEN	1:01.6	VII			
Obial	PHI	1:01.7	VI			
Fred Dove	GBR	1:01.8	VI			
Paul Schwartz	GER	1:01.8	III			
Leonard Spence	BER	1:01.9	IV			
Hammertom	CAN	1:02.1	I			
Rene Cavalero	FRA	1:02,2	II			
Munroe Bourne	CAN	1:02.4	III			
Tatto	BRA	1:02.6	I			
Francisco Marques	BRA	1:03.3	VI			
Dos Santos Moraes	BRA	1:03.5	III			
Zaki Saad el Din	EGY	1:03.7	V			
Kadri	EGY	1:03.8	I			
Gunther Zobernig	AUT	1:03.9	III			
Zirilli	SUI	1:04.1	VII			
Claude Desusclade	FRA	1:04.2	IV			
Alvarez Calderone	PER	1:04.9	I			
Pas Soldao	PER	1:05.6	V			
Chan	CHN	1:06,5	I			
Broussalis	GRE	1:07.5	IV			
Young	BER	1:07.8	VI			
Mavrogeorgos	GRE	1:08.2	V			
Conrad Muchoca	Bol	1:17.5	II			

Bertus Mooy	NED	No Time	II					
Doria	SUI	No Time	II					
Ledgard	PER	No Time	III					
Dunand	SUI	No Time	V					
Alfred Nakache	FRA	No Time	VI					
Gullini	BEL	No Time	VII					
Darko Prvan	YUG	No Time	IV					

Men's 400 Meter Freestyle:		Trial		Semi		Final	
1) Jack Medica	USA	4:55.9	VI	4:48.2	II	Lo4:44.5	
2) Shumpei Uto	JPN	o4:45.5	V	4:48.4	I	4:45.6	
3) Shozo Makino	JPN	4:51.5	III	4:48.2	II	4:48.1	
4 Ralph Flanagan	USA	4:54.7	III	4:54.9	I	4:52.7	
5 Hirosi Negami	PN	4:52.6	I	4:55.4	I	4:53.6	
6 Jean Taris	FRA	4:53.9	V	4:55.6	II	4:53.8	
7 Robert Leivers	GBR	4:57.2	II	4:55.7	II	5:00.9	
John Macionis	USA	4:57.1	I	4:56.4	I		
Hans Freesa	GER	5:03.1	IV	4:58.5	I		
Bob Pirie	CAN	4:56.0	V	4:58.7	I		
Odin Grof	HUN	4:59.4	IV	5:01.9	I		
Heinz Arendt	GER	4:57.2	I	5:13.4	II		
Otto Przywara	GER	5:11.7	II	5:14.9	II		
Arpad Lengyel	HUN	4:57.7	I				
Norman Wainwright	GBR	5:03.6	III				
Ledgard	PER	5:05.5	VI	DNS	II		
Piet Stam	NED	5:07.8	VI				
HJ Haitonen	FIN	5:08.9	IV				
W. Pearson	GBR	5:12.7	IV				
Hammerton	CAN	5:13.3	III				
Edmund Pader	AUT	5:16.9	I				
Hooper	CAN	5:17.2	I				
De Rocha Vilar	BRA	5:18.2	VI				
Aage Hellstrom	DEN	5:18.2	II				
W. Guzman	CHL	5:19.1	IV				
Poul Petersen	DEN	5:20.3	V				
Gyorgy Angyel	HUN	5:20.9	III				
Fautin Havelanger	BRA	5:31.5	II				
Brenner	SUI	5:33.8	VI				
Lehmann	SUI	5:36.8	III				
Seltenheim	AUT	5:38.3	IV				
Cooper	BER	5:53.8	V				
Zirilli	SUI	No Time	I				
Gunther Zobernig	AUT	No Time	II				
Chan	CHN	No Time	II				
Spurling	BER	No Time	II				
Jorgen Jorgensen	DEN	No Time	III				
Lage	BRA	No Time	IV				
Guzman	CHL	No Time	IV				
Poul Petersen	DEN	No Time	V				

E. Roolaid	EST	No Time	V				
Provatopoulus	GRE	No Time	V				
Kadri	EGY	No Time	VI				

Men's 1500 Meter Freestyle:		Trial		Semi		Final	
1) Norburu Terada	JPN	19:55.5	II	19:48.6	I	19:13.7	
2) Jack Medica	USA	19:55.5	II	19:42.8	II	19:34.0	
3) Shumpei Uto	JPN	19:48.3	III	19:55.6	II	19:34.5	
4 Sunao Ishiharada	JPN	19:55.8	I	19:53.9	II	19:48.5	
5 Ralph Flanagan	USA	19:49.9	III	19:59.4	I	19:54.8	
6 Robert Leivers	GBR	20:04.4	I	20:10.0	I	19:57.4	
7 Heinz Arendt	GER	20:10.7	I	19:56.1	II	19:59.0	
Norman Wainwright	GBR	20:47.6	IV	20:14.4	II		
Jim Cristy	USA	20:26.2	IV	20:25.8	I		
Hans Freese	GER	20:13.7	III	20:27.6	I		
Otto Przywara	GER	20:59.0	IV	20:55.0	I		
Christian Talli	FRA	21:09.8	III	21:09.8	II		
Jorgen Jorgensen	DEN	21:42.0	II	21:46.3	I		
Bob Pirie	CAN	20:16.4	I	20:17.3	II		
Hamerton	CAN	21:05.5	III				
Edmund Pador	AUT	21:13.9	IV				
Aage Hellstrom	DEN	21:16.9	III				
Hooper	CAN	21:47.4	I				
Da Rocha Villar	BRA	21:49.9	II				
Faustin Havelanger	BRA	22:54.1	II				
Gyorgy Angyel	HUN	No Time	I				
Kadry	EGY	No Time	I				
Patuzzi	AUT	No Time	I				
Odin Grof	HUN	No Time	II				
Guzman	CHL	No Time	II				
Garcia	URU	No Time	III				
Arpad Lengyel	HUN	No Time	IV				
Berroeta	CHL	No Time	IV				

Men's 100 Meter Backstroke:		Trial		Semi		Final	
1) Adolph Kiefer	USA	o1:06.9	I	o1:06.8	I	o1:05.9	
2) Albert Vandeweghe	USA	1:10.6	III	1:08.6	I	1:07.7	
3) Masaji Kiyokawa	JPN	1:07.2	I	1:09.7	II	1:08.4	
4 Taylor Drysdale	USA	1:09.0	II	1:08.6	II	1:09.4	
5 Kiichi Yoshida	JPN	1:10.0	V	1:09.9	I	1:09.7	
6 Yasumiko Kojima	JPN	1:09.7	III	1:09.9	II	1:10.4	
7 Percy Oliver	AUS	1:10.2	V	1:09.4	I	1:10.7	
Heinz Schlauch	GER	1:10.1	II	1:10.8	II		
Nil Christiansen	PHI	1:11.5	III	1:11.1	I		
Gordon Kerr	CAN	1:12.9	IV	1:11.2	II		
Erwin Simon	GER	1:11.7	III	1:11.7	I		
Hans Schwarz	GER	1:11.0	I	1:11.7	I		
D. Wilfan	YUG	1:11.7	II	1:13.3	II		

John Besford	GBR	1:12.0	IV	1:13.6	II
Piet Metman	NED	1:13.7	V	1:14.1	II
Gyorgy Erdelyi	HUN	1:14.7	III		
Bjorn Borg	SWE	1:15.2	IV	1:16.3	I
Arpad Lengyel	HUN	1:15.2	II		
Elemer Gombos	HUN	1:12.4	I		
Stans Scheffer	NED	1:13.6	II		
JE Middleton	GBR	1:15.0	I		
Novo Caballero	BRA	1:16.3	V		
Martins	BRA	1:16.9	I		
Munroe Bourne	CAN	1:17.2	II		
Borge Baeth	DEN	1:17.3	V		
Neumann	LUX	1:18.8	III		
Casa-Sempere	CHL	1:21.0	V		
Amaral Filho	BRA	1:21.0	II		
Roolaid	EST	1:21.1	IV		
Mallides	GRE	1:21.5	IV		
Doe	BER	No Time	I		
Martins Numes	BRA	No Time	I		
Patuzzi	AUT	No Time	III		
Carpio	PER	No Time	IV		
Mallides	GRE	No Time	IV		
Praunsperger	YUG	No Time	IV		
Cooper	BER	No Time	V		

Men's 200 Meter Breaststroke:		Trial		Semi		Final
1) Tetsuo Hamuro	JPN	o2:42.5	I	2:43.4	II	o2:42.5
2) Erwin Sietas	GER	2:44.6	I	2:44.8	II	2:42.9
3) Reizo Koike	JPN	2:43.8	V	2:44.5	I	2:44.2
4 John Higgins	USA	2:48.8	III	2:44.0	II	2:45.2
5 Saburo Ito	JPN	2:45.8	II	2:45.5	I	2:47.6
6 Joachim Balke	GER	2:46.4	II	2:45.4	I	2:47.8
7 Teofilo Yldefonzo	PHI	2:47.4	V	2:46.6	II	2:51.1
Artur Heina	GER	2:48.5	V	2:47.3	II	
Ray Kaye	USA	2:48.5	I	2:49.2	I	
Jack Kasley	USA	2:54.4	II	2:53.4	II	
F. Erbert	CZE	2:55.7	IV	2:53.5	II	
Jikirum Adjaluddin	PHI	2:50.2	I	2:54.0	I	
Leonard Spence	BER	2:52.0	IV	DQ	II	
M. Alpad	PHI	2:52.6	III	2:56.0	I	
GH Clawsen	CZE	2:54.7	IV	No Time	I	
Finn Jensen	DEN	2:55.7	III	No Time	I	
Erbert	CZE	2:55.7	IV			
Hans Malmstrom	DEN	2:56.5	V			
Dos Santos	BRA	2:56.8	III			
Skou	DEN	2:57.6	II			
Mohamed	EGY	2:58.9	III			
Arp	BRA	3:02.6	I			
Belvin	BER	3:09.8	II			

Puddy	CAN	3:10.2	II	
Keel	SUI	No Time	II	
Sandor Barocsy	HUN	No Time	I	
Schmetz	SUI	No Time	I	
Girg	AUT	No Time	V	
Zimmermann	SUI	No Time	V	
Berroeta	CHL	DQ	III	
Reed	CHL	DQ	IV	

Men's 4x200 Meter Freestyle Relay: **Trial**   **Final**

	Trial		Final
2:13.4 2:11.9 2:13.2 2:13.2			
1) JPN (Yusa Sugiura,Taguchi Arai)	o8:56.1	III	Wo8:51.5
2:15.4 2:16.0 2:16.0 2:15.4			
2) USA (Flanagan,Macionis,P.Wolf,Medica)	9:10.4	II	9:03.0
3) HUN (Grof,Lengyel,Abay-Nemes,Csik)	9:20.8	II	9:12.3
4 FRA (Nakache,Talli,Cavalero,Taris)	9:21.7	I	9:18.2
5 GER (Plath,Heibel,Heimlich,Fischer	9:21.4	III	9:19.0
6 GBR (French-Williams,Gabrielsen,Leivers,Wainwright)	9:30.8	II	9:21.5
7 CAN (Bourne,Hamerton,Hooper,Pirie)	9:40.0	I	9:27.5
8 SWE (B.Borg,Boliden,Pettersson,Werner)	9:35.3	III	9:37.5
DEN	9:39.6	II	
YUG	9:40.3	III	
BRA	9:42.5	I	
EGY	10:05.3	III	
AUT	10:58.3	II	
LUX	10:59.9	II	
BER	No Time	I	
GRE	No Time	I	
CHL	No Time	I	
PHI	No Time	I	
POL	DQ	II	

In the trial, Gilman and Hutter (USA) swam in place of Flanagan and Medica.

1936 Men's Olympic Swimming Medals

	Gold	Medals
JPN	3	10
USA	2	5
HUN	1	2
GER	0	1

1896-1936 Men's Olympic Swimming Medals

	Gold	Medals
USA	21	50
JPN	9	24
GER	8	19
GBR	6	15
HUN	5	16
AUS	4	16
SWE	3	12
CAN	2	5
AUT	1	8
FRA	1	5
ARG	1	1
GRE	0	5

BEL	0		2
DEN	0		2
FIN	0		2
PHI	0		2
NED	0		1

Women's 100 Meter Freestyle:		Trial		Semi		Final
1) Hendrika Mastenbroek	NED	o1:06.4	I	o1:06.4	I	o1:05.9
2) Jeanette Campbell	ARG	1:06.8	III	1:06.6	II	1:06.4
3) Gisela Arendt	GER	1:07.3	I	1:07.2	I	1:06.6
4 Willi den Ouden	NED	1:08.1	II	1:06.7	II	1:07.6
5 Catherina "Tini" Wagner	NED	1:08.9	III	1:08.6	I	1:08.1
6 Olive McKean	USA	1:09.3	II	1:08.9	II	1:08.4
7 Katherine Rawls	USA	1:08.8	I	1:08.5	I	1:08.7
Phyllis Dewar	CAN	1:09.2	I	1:09.6	I	
Bernice Lapp	USA	1:09.0	V	1:09.6	II	
Azeveda Coutinho	BRA	1:09.4	III	1:09.8	I	
Evelyn De Lacy	AUS	1:08.5	II	1:10.0	II	
Kasue Kojima	JPN	1:11.0	IV	1:11.1	I	
Olive Wadham	GBR	1:11.5	IV	1:12.0	II	
Magda Lenkei	HUN	1:09.9	V	1:12.1	I	
Stone	CAN	1:10.0	V	1:12.8	II	
Ragnhild Hveger	DEN	1:09.6	IV	1:14.0	II	
Eva Arndt	DEN	1:10.1	I			
Leni Lohmar	GER	1:10.3	V			
Elvi Svendsen	DEN	1:10.3	III			
Renee Blondeau	FRA	1:10.9	V			
Inge Schmitz	GER	1:10.9	III			
Vera Harsanyi	HUN	1:11.5	III			
ID Schramekova	CZE	1:11.8	IV			
Zilpha Grant	GBR	1:12.1	III			
Ilona Acs	HUN	1:12.7	II			
Irene Pirie-Milton	CAN	1:12.8	II			
Margery Hinton	GBR	1:13.0	I			
Kitty MacKay	AUS	1:13.8	IV			
Tsuneko Furuta	JPN	1:14.6	II			
Takemura	JPN	1:14.6	I			
Vernancio	BRA	1:15.1	I			
De Moracs Salles	BRA	1:16.2	IV			
Yeung	CHN	1:22.2	IV			
Klavtovska	CZE	No Time	II			
De Moraes Salles	BRA	No Time	IV			
Rademaecker	BEL	No Time	V			
Villiger	SUI	No Time	V			

Women's 400 Meter Freestyle:

			Trial		Semi		Final
1)	Hendrika Mastenbroek	NED	5:38.6	V	5:40.3	I	Lo5:26.4
2)	Ragnhild Hveger	DEN	o5:28.0	I	5:33.7	II	5:27.5
3)	Lenore Kight-Wingard	USA	5:34.0	I	5:42.2	I	#5:29.2
5	Azevedo Coutinho	BRA	5:35.5	I	5:42.3	II	5:35.2
6	Kasue Kojima	JPN	5:50.4	V	5:43.5	II	5:43.1
7	Grete Fredericksen	DEN	5:39.5	III	5:42.5	I	5:45.0
8	Catherina "Tini" Wagner	NED	5:57.5	II	5:45.9	I	5:46.0
	Schramekova	CZE	5:47.5	V	5:46.0	I	
	Hatsuko Morioka	JPN	5:51.0	III	5:49.1	I	
	Annie Timmermans	NED	5:42.5	III	5:49.4	II	
	Inger Carlsen	DEN	5:57.1	IV	5:55.0	II	
	Margaret Jeffrey	GBR	6:12.7	IV	6:07.2	II	
	Vera Harsanyi	HUN	6:14.7	I			
	Sothy	HUN	6:14.8	II	6:11.2	I	
	Evelyn DeLacy	AUS	5:51.9	III			
	Louisette Fleuret	FRA	5:56.8	III			
	Gladys Morcom	GBR	6:00.8	I			
	Agnes Biro	HUN	6:14.3	V			
	Vera Harsanyi	HUN	6:14.7	I			
	Vanancio	VEN	6:23.0	V			
	Stone	CAN	No Time	I			
	Phyllis Dewar	CAN	No Time	II			
	Dorothea Dickenson	USA	No Time	II			
	Margery Hinton	GBR	No time	II			
	De Moraes Salles	BRA	No Time	II			
	Villiger	SUI	No Time	III			
	Irene Pirie-Milton	CAN	No Time	IV			
	Yeung	CHN	No Time	IV			
	Langer	AUT	No Time	IV			
	Jeanette Campbell	ARG	No Time	V			

Unofficial time. Official time not known

Women's 100 Meter Backstroke:

			Trial		Semi		Final
1)	Dina "Nida" Senff	NED	Lo1:16.6	I	1:17.1	I	1:18.9
2)	Hendrika Mastenbroek	NED	1:22.0	III	1:19.1	II	1:19.2
3)	Alice Bridges	USA	1:19.2	II	1:20.4	II	1:19.4
4	Edith Mottridge	USA	1:21.0	III	1:19.1	I	1:19.6
5	Tove Brunstroem	DEN	1:20.4	I	1:19.7	I	1:20.4
6	Lorna Frampton	GBR	1:20.9	I	1:19.6	II	1:20.6
7	Phyllis Harding	GBR	1:22.1	II	1:19.8	I	1:21.5
	AG Kerkmeester	NED	1:21.2	II	1:21.3	II	
	AM Hancock	GBR	1:23.6	III	1:21.6	II	
	Anni Stolte	GER	1:23.1	I	1:21.7	I	
	Pat Norton	AUS	1:22.3	II	1:21.9	I	
	Tove Nielsen	DEN	1:25.3	III	1:22.0	II	
	Christel Rupke	GER	1:23.7	II			
	Therese Blondeau	FRA	1:23.8	II			
	Kitty MacKay	AUS	1:24,6	I			

McConkey	CAN	1:25.3	III
Iren Gyorfy	HUN	1:25.8	I
Roma Wagner	AUT	1:28.4	II
Oxenbury	CAN	1:28.9	I
Maria Lenk	BRA	1:32.0	I
Yeung	CHN	1:36.4	III
Irene Milton-Pirie	CAN	No Time	II

Women's 200 Meter Breaststroke:		Trial		Semi		Final
1) Hideko Maehata	JPN	Lo3:01.9	III	3:03.1	I	3:03.6
2) Martha Genenger	GER	3:03.0	II	3:02.8	II	3:04.2
3) Inge Sorensen	DEN	3:06.7	I	3:06.0	I	3:07.8
4 Johanna "Hanni" Holzner	GER	3:11.0	I	3:08.8	I	3:09.5
5 Johanna "Jopie" Waalberg	NED	3:10.4	I	3:09.7	I	3:09.5
6 Doris Storey	GBR	3:10.8	IV	3:09.8	II	3:09.7
7 Jennette"Jennie"Kastein	NED	3:07.8	II	3:09.2	II	3:12.8
Trude Wollschlager	GER	3:08.5	IV	3:10.3	I	
Kerstin Isberg	SWE	3:08.7	I	3:11.4	II	
Valborg Christensen	DEN	3:12.0	III	3:14.1	II	
MO Gomm	GBR	3:15.7	III	3:15.8	I	
Maria Lenk	BRA	3:17.2	IV	3:17.7	I	
U. Tsuboi	JPN	3:15.0	II	3:18.4	II	
Dorothy Schiller	USA	3:17.4	I	3:18.5	II	
Lappalainen	FIN	3:19.7	II			
Edle Nielsen	DEN	3:21.3	IV			
Vera Kingston	GBR	3:21.7	I			
Iris Cummings	USA	3:21.9	III			
Stroomberg	NED	3:22.5	IV			
J. Langdon	CAN	3:24.3	I			
Anne Godvednik	USA	3:25.3	II			
Boubelova	CZE	3:25.8	III			
Wyss	SUI	3:31.3	III			
Fraudenreich	AUT	No Time	II			
Steiner	AUT	No Time	IV			

Women's 4x100 Meter Freestyle Relay:	Trial		Final
1) NED (Selbach,Wagner,denOuden,Mastenbroek)	4:38.1	II	Lo4:36.0
2) GER (Halbsguth,Lohmar,Schmitz,Arendt)	4:40.5	II	4:36.8
3)USA (Rawls,Lapp,Freeman,McKean)	4:47.1	I	4:40.2
4 HUN (Acs,Biro Harsany,Lenkei	4:50.6	I	4:48.0
5 CAN (McConkey,Pirie-Milton,Stone,Dewar)	4:49.7	I	4:48.0
6 GBR (Grant,Hughes,Jeffrey,Wadham)	4:47.2	I	4:51.0
7 DEN (Hveger,Bruunstrom,Svendsen,Arndt)	4:46.2	II	4:51.4
JPN	4:58.1	II	
AUT	5:16.6	I	

In the Trial Ursula Pollack swam in place of Arendt for GER and Elizabeth Ryan swam in place of McKean for USA.

W World Record, L World Long Course Best, o Olympic Record

200 m back (3:10.4, 1906; 3:08.8, Hanover, 1908)
International Swimming Hall of Fame (1988)

BLEIBTREY, ETHELDA (1902-1978), USA (WOMEN'S SA, AMBASSADOR SC)
50 yd free through mile, 100 through 150 yd back (1919-22)
Olympics (1):
 Antwerp 1920: 100 m free (1st, 1:13.6), 300 m free (1st, 4:34.0), 4 x 100 m free relay (1st, 5:11.6)
World Records (7):
 100 yd free (1:03.8, New Brighton, 1921, 25 yd)
 100 m free (1:13.6, Antwerp, 1920, 100 m)
 300 yd free (4:18.6, Indianapolis, 1921, 100 yd)
 300 m free (4:34.0, Antwerp, 1920, 100 m)
 400 m free (6:30.2, New York City, 1919, 100 yd)
 440 yd free (6:30.2, New York City, 1919, 110 yd)
 150 yd back (2:10.2, Jersey City, 1920, 33.3 yd)
World Long Course Best Times (9):
 100 m free (1920)
 200 m free (1920-21)
 400 m free (1919-21)
 800 m free (1919, 21)
 100 m back (1919)
National Titles (NAAU Outdoor) (9):
 50 yd free (1921), 100 yd free (1920-21), 440 yd free (1919, 21), 880 yd free (1919-21),
  mile free (1920)
National Titles (NAAU Indoor) (5):
 50 yd free (1920), 100 yd free (1920, 22), 500 yd free (1919), 100 yd back (1920)
International Swimming Hall of Fame (1967)

BLITZ, GERARD (1901-1979), BEL
100 through 400 m back (1920-28)
Olympics (3):
 Antwerp 1920: 100 m back (3rd, 1:19.0)
 Paris 1924: 100 m back (4th, 1:19.6)
 Amsterdam 1928: 100 m back (scratched semi after heat, 1:18.8)
World Records (1):
 400 m back (5:59.2, Exeter, 1921, 25 yd)

BOARDMAN, LESLIE (1889-?), AUS
100 through 220 yd free
Olympics (1):
 Stockholm 1912: 100 m free (eliminated in second round, 1:05.4), 4 x 200 m free relay (1st,
  10:11.2, as Australasia)

BORG, ARNE (1901-1987), SWE (SKK, ILL. AC)
100 m free through mile (1919-29)
Olympics (3):
 Antwerp 1920: 1500 m free (eliminated in heat, 23:53.0), 4 x 200 m free relay (4th, 10:50.2)
 Paris 1924: 100 m free (4th, 1:02.0), 400 m free (2nd, 5:05.6), 1500 m free (2nd, 20:41.4),
  4 x 200 m free relay (3rd, 10:06.8)
 Amsterdam 1928: 400 m free (3rd, 5:04.6), 1500 m free (1st, 19:51.8), 4 x 200 m free relay (5th,
  10:01.8)
World Records (34):
 300 yd free (3:16.4, Stockholm, 1925, 25 yd)
 300 m free (3:33.8, Stockholm, 1925, 25 yd; 3:33.5, Stockholm, 1926, 25 yd; 3:28.1, Stockholm,

1927, 25 yd)

400 m free (5:11.8, Stockholm, 1922, 25 yd; 4:54.7, Stockholm, 1924, 25 yd; 4:50.3, Stockholm, 1925, 25 yd)

440 yd free (5:11.8, Stockholm, 1922, 25 yd; 4:52.6, Stockholm, 1925, 25 yd)

500 yd free (5:38.1, Stockholm, 1925, 25 yd; 5:31.4, Detroit, 1926, 25 yd)

500 m free (6:32.9, Stockholm, 1922, 25 yd; 6:19.7, Stockholm, 1924, 25 yd; 6:08.4, Stockholm, 1925, 25 yd)

800 m free (10:43.6, Honolulu, 1924, 50 m; 10:37.4, Harnus, 1925, 50 m)

880 yd free (10:43.6, Honolulu, 1924, 50 m; 10:37.4, Harnus, 1925, 50 m)

1000 yd free (13:15.7, Goteborg, 1922, 50 m; 12:47.8, Goteborg, 1923, 50 m; 12:16.8, Goteborg, 1924, 50 m; 11:55.4, Sydney, 1929, 55 yd)

1000 m free (14:18.3, Christiana, 1921, 50 m; 14:00.3, Goteborg, 1923, 50 m; 13:04.2, Oslo, 1925, 50 m; 13:02.0, Budapest, 1928, 50 m)

1500 m. free (21:35.3, Goteborg, 1923, 50 m; 21:15.0, Sydney, 1924, 110 yd; 21:11.4, Paris, 1924, 50 m; 20:04.4, Budapest, 1926, 50 m; 19:07.2, Bologna, 1927, 50 m)

Mile free (22:34.0, Sydney, 1924, 110 yd; 21:41.3, Goteborg, 1925, 50 m; 21:06.8, Sydney, 1929, 55 yd)

World Long Course Best Times (23):

400 m free (4:59.0, Honolulu, 1924)

800 m free (10:43.6, Honolulu, 1924; 10:37.4, Harnas, 1925; 10:31.0, Budapest, 1926; 10:09.0, Bologna, 1927)

880 yd free (10:42.6, Honolulu, 1924; 10:37.4, Harnas, 1925)

1000 yd free (13:15.7, Goteborg, 1922; 12:47.8, Goteborg, 1923; 12:16.8, Goteborg, 1924; 11:55.4, Sydney, 1929)

1000 m free (14:18.3, Christiania, 1921; 14:00.3, Goteborg, 1923; 13:04.2, Oslo, 1925; 13:02.0, Budapest, 1928)

1500 m free (21:35.3, Goteborg, 1923; 21:15.0, Sydney, 1924; 21:11.4, Paris, 1924; 20:04.8, Budapest, 1926; 19:07.2, Bologna, 1927)

Mile free (22:34.0, Sydney, 1924; 21:41.3, Goteborg, 1925; 21:06.8, Sydney, 1929)

European Championships (2):

Budapest 1926: 100 m free (2nd, 1:01.2), 400 m free (1st, 5:14.2), 1500 m free (1st, 21:29.2), 4 x 200 m free relay (3rd, 10:06.8)

Bologna 1927: 100 m free (1st, 1:00.0), 400 m free (1st, 5:08.6), 1500 m free (1st, 19:07.2), 4 x 200 m free relay (2nd, 9:50.0)

National Titles (29):

100 m free (1923, 25, 27-29), 200 m free (1920-22, 24-25, 27-29), 500 m free (1919-24, 27-28), 1500 m free (1920-23, 27-28), 100 m back (1923)

USA National Titles (NAAU Outdoor) (2):

800 m free (1926), mile free (1926)

USA National Titles (NAAU Indoor) (4):

220 yd free (1925-26), 500 yd free (1925-26)

International Swimming Hall of Fame (1966)

BRACK, WALTER (1880-1919), GER

100 yd back, 440 yd breast (1904)

Olympics (1):

St. Louis 1904: 100 yd back (1st, 1:16.8), 440 yd breast (2nd, 7:33.0)

International Swimming Hall of Fame (1997)

BRAUN, MARIE (1911-1982), NED (ODZ)

100 through 400 m free, 100 through 400 m back (1926-32)

Olympics (2):

Amsterdam 1928: 400 m free (2nd, 5:57.8), 100 m back (1st, 1:22.0), 4 x 100 m free relay (DQ; 2nd qualifier in heat, 5:08.8)

Los Angeles 1932: 400 m free (eliminated in heat, 5:50.5), 100 m back (eliminated in heat, 1:23.8)

World Records (6):

500 m free (7:18.0, Bruges, 1930, 25 m)

100 m back (1:21.6, Amsterdam, 1928, 50 m; 1:21.4, Brussels, 1929, 25 m; 1:21.0, Den Haag, 1929, 25 m)

200 m back (2:59.2, Brussels, 1928, 25 m)

400 m back (6:16.8, Paris, 1930, 25 m)

World Long Course Best Times (1):

100 m back (1:21.6, Amsterdam, 1928)

European Championships (2):

Bologna 1927: 100 m free (6th, 1:18.0), 400 m free (1st, 6:11.8), 100 m back (2nd, 1:26.2), 4 x 100 m free relay (2nd, 5:11.0)

Paris 1931: 400 m free (1st, 5:42.0), 100 m back (2nd, 1:22.8), 4 x 100 m free relay (1st, 4:55.0)

National Titles (4):

400 m free (1927), 100 m back (1927, 29, 32)

BREYER, RALPH (1904-1991), USA (CHICAGO AA, NORTHWESTERN UNIV.)

50 yd through 400 m free (1924-26)

Olympics (1):

Paris 1924: 4 x 200 m free relay (1st, 9:53.4)

NCAA Titles (3):

50 yd free (1925), 100 yd free (1924-25), 220 yd free (1924)

BRIDGES, ALICE (1916-   ), USA (WHITINSVILLE, CALIF.)

100 through 220 yd free, 100 through 220 yd back (1933-36)

Olympics (1):

Berlin 1936: 100 m back (3rd, 1:19.4)

World Records (1):

150 yd back (1:50.8, Brunswick, 1935, 25 yd)

National Titles (NAAU Outdoor) (1):

220 yd back (1934)

BROCKWAY, JOHN (1928-   ), WAL (MAINDEE ASC)

100 through 220 yd back (1948-56)

Olympics (3):

London 1948: 100 m back (7th, 1:09.2)

Helsinki 1952: 100 m back (eliminated in semi, 1:09.0)

Melbourne 1956: 100 m back (eliminated in heat, 1:07.7)

European Championships (1):

Torino 1954: 100 m back (3rd, 1:05.9)

Empire Games (1):

Auckland 1950: 110 yd back (2nd, 1:08.0)

Commonwealth Games (1):

Vancouver 1954: 110 yd back (1st, 1:06.5)

English ASA Titles (7):

100 yd back (1948-51), 110 yd back (1953-55)

BURKE, LYNN (1943-   ), USA (FLUSHING Y, SANTA CLARA SC)

100 through 200 m back (1959-60)

Olympics (1):

Rome 1960: 100 m back (1st, 1:09.3), 4 x 100 medley relay (1st, 4:41.4, back leg, 1:09.0)

World Records and World Long Course Best Times (6):

100 m back (1:10.7, Indianapolis, 1960; 1:10.1, Indianapolis, 1960; 1:10.0, Detroit, 1960;

1:09.2, Detroit, 1960; 1:09.0, Rome, 1960)
200 m back (2:33.5, Indianapolis, 1960)
Pan Am Games (1):
Chicago 1959: 100 m back (4th, 1:13.8)
National Titles (NAAU Outdoor) (2):
100 m back (1960), 200 m back (1960)
National Titles (NAAU Indoor) (2):
100 yd back (1960), 150 yd back (1960)
International Swimming Hall of Fame (1978)

CAMPBELL, JEANETTE (1916-2003), ARG
100 through 400 m free (1935-39)
Olympics (1):
Berlin 1936: 100 m free (2nd, 1:06.4)
South American Championships (3):
Rio de Janeiro 1935: 100 m free (1st, 1:08.0), 400 m free (1st, 5:47.8)
Montevideo 1937: 100 m free (1st, 1:06.7), 400 m free (2nd, 5:34.0)
Buenos Aires 1938: 100 m free (1st, 1:07.0)
International Swimming Hall of Fame (1991)

CARSON, GLADYS (1905-1997), ENG (LEICESTER LADIES)
200 yd and 200 m breast (1921-24)
Olympics (1):
Paris 1924: 200 m breast (3rd, 3:35.4; 3:30.0 in heat)
English ASA Titles (1): 200 yd breast (3:12.4, 1924)

CARTER, KEITH (1924-   ), USA (PURDUE UNIV., LAFAYETTE SC)
50 yd through 100 m free, 100 through 220 yd breast, 150 yd IM (1947-49)
Olympics (1):
London 1948: 100 m free (4th, 58.3), 200 m breast (2nd, 2:40.2)
World Records (3):
100 yd breast (1:00.1, Lafayette, 1947, 25 yd; 59.4, Lafayette, 1948, 25 yd; 58.5, Lafayette, 1949, 25 yd)
National Titles (NAAU Indoor) (1):
220 yd breast (1949)
NCAA Titles (1):
200 yd breast (1949)

CEDERQUIST, JANE (1945-   ), SWE (NEPTUN)
400 through 1500 m free (1958-61)
Olympics (1):
Rome 1960: 400 m free (2nd, 4:53.9)
World Records and World Long Course Best Times (2):
800 m free (9:55.6, Uppsala, 1960)
1500 m free (19:23.6, Uppsala, 1960)

CHAMPION, MALCOLM (1896-1948), NZL
200 through 1500 m free (1912)
Olympics (1):
Stockholm 1912: 400 m free (eliminated in semi, 5:38.0), 1500 m free (dropped out of final at 600 meters), 4 x 200 m free relay (1st, 10:11.2, as Australasia, 2nd leg, 2:33.5)

CHARLTON, ANDREW "BOY" (1907-1975), AUS
200 m free through mile (1923-35)

Olympics (3):
  Paris 1924: 1500 m free (1st, 20:06.6), 400 m free (3rd, 5:06.6), 4 x 200 m free relay (2nd, 10:02.2)
  Amsterdam 1928: 400 m free (2nd, 5:03.6), 1500 m free (2nd, 20:02.6)
  Los Angeles 1932): 400 m free (6th, 4:58.6), 1500 m free (eliminated in semi, 19:53.1; 5th fastest time in semi, but 4th in heat)
World Records (8):
  800 m and 880 yd free (11:05.2sy, Sydney, 1923; 10:51.8sy, Sydney, 1924; 10:32.0, Harnas, 1927)
  1000 m free (13:19.5, Paris, 1924)
  1500 m free (20:06.6, Paris, 1924)
World Long Course Best Times (3):
  800 m free (11:05.2sy, Sydney, 1923; 10:51.8sy, Sydney, 1924)
  1500 m free (20:06.6, Paris, 1924)
New South Wales Titles (12):
  mile free, 2 x 220 yd free relay, 4 x 440 yd free relay, 4 x 880 yd free relay (1923-35)
International Swimming Hall of Fame (1972)

CLAPP, AUSTIN (1910-1972), USA (HOLLYWOOD AC, STANFORD UNIV.)
200 m free through mile, 300 through 330 yd IM (1928-32)
Olympics (1):
  Amsterdam 1928: 400 m free (5th, 5:16.0), 1500 m free (eliminated in heat, 21:31.0), 4 x 200 m free relay (1st, 9:10.5)
NCAA Titles (1):
  220 yd free (2:18.0, 1931)

COOPER, JOYCE (1909-2002), ENG (MERMAID CLUB)
100 through 440 yd free, 100 m and 150 yd back
Olympics (2):
  Amsterdam 1928: 100 m free (3rd, 1:13.6), 100 m back (3rd, 1:22.8), 4 x 100 m free relay (2nd, 5:02.8)
  Los Angeles 1932: 100 m free (eliminated in semi, 1:09.2), 400 m free (4th, 5:49.7),
  100 m back (6th, 1:23.4), 4 x 100 m free relay (3rd, 4:52.4)
World Records (1):
  150 yd back (1:54.0, Glasgow, 1931, 25 yd)
European Championships (2):
  Bologna 1927: 100 m free (2nd, 1:15.1), 4 x 100 m free relay (1st, 5:11.0)
  Paris 1931: 100 m free (3rd, 1:12.0), 400 m free (5:54.0, 2nd), 100 m back (2nd, 1:23.6), 4 x 100 m free relay (1st, 5:00.8)
Empire Games (1):
  Hamilton 1930: 100 yd free (1st, 1:07.0), 400 yd free (1st, 5:25.4), 100 yd back (1st, 1:15.0), 4 x 100 yd free relay (1st, 4:32.8, 25 yd)
English ASA Titles (19):
  100 yd free (1929, 31-32), 220 yd free (1927-29, 31-32), 440 yd free (1928-32), 150 yd back (1929, 31), long distance (1930-33)
International Swimming Hall of Fame (1996)

COURTMAN, PERCY (1888-1917), ENG (OLD TRAFFORD ASC)
200 yd through 400 m breast (1907-14)
Olympics (2):
  London 1908: 200 m breast (eliminated in heat, 3:18.4)
  Stockholm 1912: 200 m breast (4th, 3:08.8), 400 m breast (3rd, 6:36.4)
World Records (3):
  200 m breast (2:56.6, Garston, 1914, 25 yd)
  400 m breast (6:14.4, Manchester, 1912, 25 yd)

500 m breast (7:51.0, Manchester, 1912, 25 yd)
English ASA Titles (5):
200 yd breast (1907-09, 12-13

COWELLS-SCHROTH, FRANCES (1893-?), USA (OAKLAND AC)
100 m free through mile (1916-24)
Olympics (1):
Antwerp 1920: 100 m free (3rd, 1:17.2), 300 m free (3rd, 4:52.0), 4 x 100 m free relay (1st, 5:11.6)
Paris 1924: qualified as an alternate
National Titles (NAAU Outdoor) (1):
mile free (1918)

CRABBE, CLARENCE "BUSTER" (1907-1983), USA (OUTRIGGER CLUB, HONOLULU CEN. Y, USC, LAAC)
220 yd free through mile, 300 through 330 yd IM (1927-32)
Olympics (2):
Amsterdam 1928: 400 m free (4th, 5:05.4), 1500 m free (3rd, 20:28.8)
Los Angeles 1932: 400 m free (1st, 4:48.4), 1500 m free (5th, 20:02.7)
World Records (1):
880 yd free (10:20.4, Long Beach, 1930, 55 yd)
U.S. Olympic Tryouts (Four firsts in 1932):
Detroit 1932: 400 m free (1st, 5:10.8), 1500 m free (1st, 20:49.6)
Cincinnati 1932: 400 m free (1st, 4:46.4), 1500 m free (1st, 20:19.2)
National Titles (NAAU Outdoor) (16):
440 yd free (1929, 31), 880 yd free (1927-31), mile free (1927-31), 330 yd IM (1928-31)
National Titles (NAAU Indoor) (7):
220 yd free (1930), 500 yd free (1930, 32), 1500 m free (1932), 300 yd IM (1930-32)
NCAA Titles (1):
440 yd free (1931)
International Swimming Hall of Fame (1965)

CRISTY, JAMES (1913-1989), USA (UNIV. OF MICHIGAN, LAKE SHORE AC)
220 yd through 1500 m free (1932-36)
Olympics (2):
Los Angeles 1932: 1500 m free (3rd, 19:39.5)
Berlin 1936: 1500 m free (eliminated in semi, 20:25.8)

CSIK, FERENC (1913-1945), HUN (BEAC)
100 and 200 m free, 100 and 200 m breast, 300 m IM (1933-38)
Olympics (1):
Berlin 1936: 100 m free (1st, 57.6), 4 x 200 m free relay (3rd, 9:12.3)
European Championships (1):
Magdeburg 1934: 100 m free (1st, 59.7), 4 x 200 m free relay (1st, 9:30.2)
National Titles (13):
100 m free (1934-38), 200 m free (1934-36), 100 m breast (1935-36), 200 m breast (1935), 300 m IM (1937)
International Swimming Hall of Fame (1983)
Physician killed in air raid

DAM, LUDVIG (1884-1972), DEN (SKK)
100 m back (1908)
Olympics (1):
London 1908: 100 m back (2nd, 1:26.6)

DANIELS, CHARLES (1885-1973), USA (NYAC)
50 yd free through mile (1904-11)
Olympics (2):
> St. Louis 1904: 50 yd free (3rd, no time), 100 yd free (2nd, no time), 220 yd free (1st, 2:44.2), 440 yd free (1st, 6:16.2)
> London 1908: 100 m free (1st, 1:05.4), 4 x 200 m free relay (3rd, 11:02.8)

Interim Games (1):
> Athens 1906: 100 m free (1st, 1:13.5)

World Records (8):
> 100 yd free (55.4, Manchester, 1907, 25 yd; 54.8, Chicago, 1910, 25 yd)
> 100 m free (1:05.6, London, 1908, 100 m; 1:02.8, New York, 1910, 25 yd)
> 200 m free (2:25.4, Pittsburg, 1911, 30 yd)
> 220 yd free (2:25.4, Pittsburg, 1909, 26.66 yd)
> 300 m free (3:57.6, New York, 1910, 25 yd)
> 500 m free (7:03.4, New York, 1907, 25 yd)

National Titles (NAAU Outdoor) (20):
> 100 yd free (1:03.8, 1905; 1:00.0, 1906; 1:03.4, 1907; 57.2, 1908), 220 yd free (2:44.2, 1904; 2:45.0, 1905; 2:42.4, 1906; 3:13.8, 1907; 2:36.8, 1908), 440 yd free (6:16.2, 1904; 6:22.0, 1905; 6:24.0, 1906; 6:26.8, 1907; 5:54.2, 1908; 5:57.4, 1909; 5:59.8, 1910), 880 yd free (12:58.6, 1905; 12:58.4, 1909), mile free (26:19.6, 1907; 27:20.6, 1908)

National Titles (NAAU Indoor) (14):
> 50 yd free (25.4, 1906; 25.2, 1909; 24.6, 1910), 100 yd free (56.6, 1909; 54.8, 1910; 56.8, 1911), 220 yd free (2:25.4, 1909; 2:33.0, 1910; 2:26.0, 1911), 440 yd free (5:50.4, 1906), 500 yd free (6:45.6, 1909; 6:28.0, 1910; 6:29.2, 1911), 880 yd free (12:29.4, 1906).

International Swimming Hall of Fame (1965)

DAVIES, VALERIE (1912-2001), WAL (ROATH PARK SC)
100 m through 440 yd free, 100 m back (1927-34)
Olympics (1):
> Los Angeles 1932: 100 m free (eliminated in heat, 1:12.7), 100 m back (3rd, 1:22.5), 4 x 100 m free relay (3rd, 4:52.4)

European Championships (3):
> Bologna 1927: 100 m back (5th, 1:33.2), 4 x 100 m free relay (1st, 5:11.0)
> Paris 1931: 400 m free (5th, 6:22.0), 4 x 100 m free relay (2nd, 5:00.8)
> Magdeburg 1934: 100 m back (eliminated in heat, 1:25.3)

Empire Games (2):
> Hamilton 1930: 100 yd free (3rd, no time), 400 yd free (2nd, 5:28.0)
> London 1934: 100 yd back (3rd, 1:18.2), 3 x 100 yd medley relay (5th, 4:01.0), 4 x 100 yd free relay (5th, 5:12.8)

DE COMBE, JOSEPH (1901-1965), BEL
200 m breast (1924-27)
Olympics (1):
> Paris 1924: 200 m breast (2nd, 2:59.2)

European Championships (1):
> Bologna 1927: 200 m breast (5th, 3:00.6)

DEN OUDEN, WILHELMINA "WILLY" (1918-1997), NED (RDZ)
100 yd through 500 m free (1931-36)
Olympics (2):
> Los Angeles 1932: 100 m free (2nd, 1:07.8), 4 x 100 m free relay (2nd, 4:47.5)
> Berlin 1936: 100 m free (4th, 1:07.6), 4 x 100 m free relay (1st, 4:36.0)

World Records (13):
> 100 yd free (59.8, Copenhagen, 1934, 25 m)

100 m free (1:06.0, Antwerp, 1933, 33.3 m; 1:05.4, Amsterdam, 1934, 25 m; 1:04.8, Rotterdam, 1934, 25 m; 1:04.6, Amsterdam, 1936, 25 m)
200 m free (2:28.6, Rotterdam, 1933, 25 m; 2:25.3, Copenhagen, 1935, 25 m)
220 yd free (2:27.6, Dundee, 1934, 25 yd)
300 yd free (3:27.0, Dundee, 1934, 25 yd)
300 m free (3:58.0, Rotterdam, 1933, 25 m; 3:50.4, Copenhagen, 1934, 25 m)
400 m free (5:16.0, Rotterdam, 1934, 25 m)
500 m free (6:48.4, Rotterdam, 1935, 25 m)

World Long Course Best Times (8):
100 m free (1:07.6, Los Angeles, 1932; 1:06.2, Budapest, 1934; 1:06.2, Schiebreck, 1934; 1:06.2, Sittard, 1934; 1:05.3, Bruxelles, 1935; 1:05.2, Doorwerth, 1935)
200 m free (2:30.4, Vienna, 1934)
400 m free (5:27.4, Magdeburg, 1934)

European Championships (2):
Paris 1931: 100 m free (2nd, 1:11.8), 4 x 100 m free relay (1st, 4:55.0)
Magdeburg 1934: 100 m free (1st, 1:07.1), 400 m free (tie for 1st, 5:27.4), 4 x 100 m free relay (1st, 4:41.5)

National Titles (5):
100 m free (1931-35)

International Swimming Hall of Fame (1970)

DE VENDEVILLE, CHARLES (? - ?), FRA
Underwater swim for distance and time (1900)
Olympics (1):
Paris 1900: underwater swim for distance and time (1st, 188.4 points)

DERBYSHIRE, ROB (1878-1938), ENG (OSBORNE ASC)
100 through 500 yd free (1897-1908)
Olympics (1):
London 1908: 100 m free (eliminated in heat, 1:12.6), 4 x 200 m free relay (1st, 10:55.6)
Interim Games (1):
Athens 1906: 4 x 300 m free relay (3rd, no time)
English ASA Titles (11):
100 yd free (1898-1901, 03-04), 220 yd free (1898, 1900-01, 03), 500 yd free (1897)

DENNIS, CLARE (1916-1971), AUS (NEW SOUTH WALES, SYDNEY LADIES CLUB)
100 m through 220 yd breast, 220 yd breast (1931-36)
Olympics (1):
Los Angeles 1932: 200 m breast (1st, 3:06.3)
World Records (2):
100 m breast (1:24.6, Unley, 1933, 33.3 yd)
200 m breast (3:08.4, Sydney, 1932, 25 m)
World Long Course Best Times (2):
200 m breast (3:08.2, Los Angeles, 1932; 3:06.3, Los Angeles, 1932)
Empire Games (1):
London 1934: 200 yd breast (1st, 2:50.2)
National Titles (4):
220 yd breast (1931, 33-35)
New South Wales Titles (3):
220 yd breast (1933-36)
International Swimming Hall of Fame (1982)

DONNELLY, EUPHRASIA (1906-), USA (HOOSIER AC)
50 yd through 440 yd free (1921-25)

Olympics (1):
    Paris 1924: 4 x 100 m free relay (1st, 4:58.8)

DOVE, FRED (? - ?), ENG (OTTER ASC)
100 through 220 yd free (1936-39)
Olympics (1):
    Berlin 1936: 100 m free (eliminated in heat, 1:01.8)
European Championships (1):
    London 1938: 100 m free (2nd, 1:00.6), 4 x 200 m free relay (3rd, 9:24.6)
Empire Games (1):
    Sydney 1938: 4 x 220 yd free relay (1st, 9:19.0), 3 x 110 yd medley relay (3:28.2)
English ASA Titles (3):
    100 yd free

DROST, JOHAN (1880-1954), NED
200 m back (1900)
Olympics (1):
    Paris 1900: 200 m back (3rd, 3:01.0)

DURACK, FANNY (1889-1969), AUS (NEW SOUTH WALES, EAST SYDNEY SC)
100 yd free through mile and breast (1906-15)
Olympics (1):
    Stockholm 1912: 100 m free (1st, 1:22.2)
World Records (9):
    100 yd free (1:06.0s, Sydney, 1912)
    100 m free (1:19.8, Stockholm, 1912; 1:18.8s, Hamburg, 1912; 1:16.2s, Sydney, 1916)
    220 yd free (2:56.0sy, Manly, 1915)
    300 m free (4:43.6s, Stockholm, 1912)
    500 yd free (7:32.4s, Newcastle, 1918; 7:08.2s, Adelaide, 1918)
    Mile free (26:08.0s, Sydney, 1914)
World Long Course Best Times (9):
    100 m free (1:19.8s, Stockholm, 1912; 1:18.8s, Hamburg, 1912; 1:17.0sy, Sydney, 1913; 1:16.2sy, Sydney, 1915)
    200 m free (2:59.0sy, Sydney, 1912; 2:56.0sy, Manly, 1915)
    400 m free (6:52.0sy, 1912; 6:03.4sy, Sydney, 1917)
    Mile free (26:08.0s, Sydney, 1914)
International Swimming Hall of Fame (1967)

EDERLE, GERTRUDE (1906-2003), USA (WOMEN'S SA)
50 through 880 yd free (1922-25)
Olympics (1):
    Paris 1920: 100 m free (3rd, 1:14.2), 400 m free (3rd, 6:04.8), 4 x 200 m free relay
    (1st, 4:58.8)
World Records (10):
    100 m free (1:12.8, Newark, 1923, 66 yd)
    200 m free (2:45.2, Brooklyn, 1923, 25 yd)
    220 yd free (2:46.8, Brooklyn, 1923, 25 yd)
    300 yd free (3:58.4, New Brighton, 1922, 25 yd)
    400 m free (5:53.2, Indianapolis, 1922, 100 yd)
    440 yd free (5:54.6, Indianapolis, 1922, 100 yd)
    500 yd free (6:45.2, Indianapolis, 1922, 100 yd)
    500 m free (7:22.2, Indianapolis, 1922, 100 yd)
    800 m free (13:19.0, Indianapolis, 1919, 110 yd)
    880 yd free (13:19.0, Indianapolis, 1919, 110 yd)

World Long Course Best Times (7):
 200 m free (1922-23)
 400 m free (1922-24)
 800 m free (1923-24)
National Titles (NAAU Outdoor) (7):
 50 yd free (1923), 220 yd free (1922-23), 440 yd free (1922-23), 880 yd free (1923-24)
National Titles (NAAU Indoor) (3):
 50 yd free (1924), 220 yd free (1923), 500 yd free (1923)
International Swimming Hall of Fame (1965)

FAHR, OTTO (1892-1969), GER (SV CANNSTATT)
1500 m free, 100 and 200 m back (1911-12)
Olympics (1):
 Stockholm 1912: 100 m back (2nd, 1:22.4)
World Records (2):
 100 m back (1:15.6, Magdeburg, 1912, 25 m)
 200 m back (2:48.4, Magdeburg, 1912, 25 m)
National Titles (1): 1500 m free (Berlin, 1911)

FARRELL, JEFFREY "JEFF" (1937-   ), USA (WICHITA SC, UNIV. OF OKLAHOMA, U.S. NAVY, NEW HAVEN SC)
50 through 220 yd free (1955-60)
Olympics (1):
 Rome 1960: 4 x 200 m free relay (1st, 8:10.2, 4th leg, 2:02.0), 4 x 100 m medley relay (1st, 4:05.4, free leg, 54.9)
World Records (Relay) (3):
 4 x 100 m free relay (3:44.4, Tokyo, 1959, 3rd leg)
 4 x 200 m free relay (8:10.2, Rome, 1960, 4th leg, 2:02.0)
 4 x 100 m medley relay (4:05.4, Rome, 1960, free leg, 54.9)
USA vs Japan (1):
 Tokyo 1959: 100 m free (1st, 56.1), 200 m free (4th, 2:08.3), 4 x 100 m free relay (1st, 3:44.4, 3rd leg), 4 x 200 m free relay (2nd, 8:31.2, 2nd leg)
National Titles (NAAU Outdoor) (4):
 100 m free (56.9, 1959; 54.8, 1960), 200 m free (2:06.9, 1959; 2:03.2, 1960)
National Titles (NAAU Indoor) (2):
 100 yd free (48.2, 1960), 220 yd free (2:00.2, 1960)
International Swimming Hall of Fame (1968)

FERGUSON, CATHY (1948-   ), USA (BURBANK Y, LOS ANGELES AC)
100 yd through 1500 m free, 100 yd through 200 m back, 200 yd through 400 m IM (1961-66)
Olympics (1):
 Tokyo 1964: 100 m back (1st, 1:07.7), 4 x 100 m medley relay (1st, 4:33.9, back leg, 1:08.6)
World Records and World Long Course Best Times (2):
 100 m back (1:07.7, Tokyo, 1964)
 200 m back (2:27.4, Los Angeles, 1964)
Pan Am Games (1):
 São Paulo 1963: 100 m back (2nd, 1:13.1)
National Titles (NAAU Outdoor) (3):
 100 and 200 m back (1963-64)
National Titles (NAAU Indoor) (2):
 100 and 200 yd back (1964)
International Swimming Hall of Fame (1978)

FINNERAN, SHARON (1946-   ), USA (CORAL GABLES SC, LOS ANGELES AC, SANTA CLARA SC)
400 m through 1650 yd free, 200 yd and 200 m fly, 400 yd and 400 m IM
Olympics (1):
   Tokyo 1964: 400 m IM (2nd, 5:24.1)
World Records and World Long Course Best Times (5):
   800 m free (9:36.9, Los Angeles, 1964)
   200 m fly (2:31.2, Chicago, 1962; 2:30.7, Los Altos, 1962, 20 m)
   400 m IM (5:27.4, Osaka, 1962; 5:21.9, Osaka, 1962)
National Titles (NAAU Outdoor) (3):
   200 m fly and 400 m IM (1962-63)
National Titles (NAAU Indoor) (4):
   500 and 1650 yd free, 200 yd fly and 400 yd IM (1962-64)
International Swimming Hall of Fame (1985)

FLETCHER, JENNIE (1890-1967), ENG (LEICESTER SC)
100 yd and 100 m free (1906-12)
Olympics (1):
   Stockholm 1912: 100 m free (3rd, 1:27.0), 4 x 100 m free relay (1st, 5:52.8)
World Records (1):
   100 yd free (1:13.6, Manchester, 1909, 25 yd)
English ASA Titles (6):
   100 yd free (1906-09, 11-12)
International Swimming Hall of Fame (1971)

FOSTER, WILLIAM (1890-1963), ENG (BACUP ASC)
200 through 1500 m free (1908-12)
Olympics (2):
   London 1908: 400 m free (4th, no time), 1500 m free (eliminated in semi, no time), 4 x 200 m
      free relay (1st, 10:55.6)
   Stockholm 1912: 400 m free (eliminated in semi, 5:49.0), 1500 m free (eliminated in semi,
      23:32.2), 4 x 200 m free relay (3rd, 10:28.2)

FRANCIS, WILLY (? - ?), SCO (RENFREW ASC)
100 through 150 yd back (1928-34)
Olympics (2):
   Amsterdam 1928: 100 m back (eliminated in semi, no time)
   Los Angeles 1932: 100 m back (eliminated in heat, 1:12.9)
European Championships (1):
   Magdeburg 1934: 100 m back (6th, 1:14.5)
Empire Games (2):
   Hamilton 1930: 100 yd back (2nd, 1:05.8)
   London 1934: 100 yd back (1st, 1:05.2), 3 x 100 yd medley relay (2nd, 3:15.2)
English ASA Titles (2): 150 yd back (1933-34)

GAILEY, FRANCIS (1882-1972), USA (OLYMPIC CLUB)
220 yd free through mile (1904)
Olympics (1):
   St. Louis 1904: 220 yd free (2nd, 2:46.0), 440 yd free (2nd, 6:22.0), 880 yd free (2nd, 13:23.4),
mile free (3rd, 28:54.0)

GARATTI-SEVILLE, ELEANOR (1909-1998), USA (SAN RAFAEL SC)
50 through 110 yd free (1925-1932)
Olympics (2):

Amsterdam 1928: 100 m free (2nd, 1:11.4), 4 x 100 m free relay (1st, 4:47.6)
Los Angeles 1932: 100 m free (3rd, 1:08.2), 4 x 100 m free relay (1st, 4:38.0)
World Records (1):
100 m free (1:09.8, Honolulu, 1929, 55 yd)
National Titles (NAAU Outdoor) (2):
110 yd free (1928-29)
National Titles (NAAU Indoor) (2):
50 yd free (1925-26)
International Swimming Hall of Fame (1992)

GENENGER, MARTHA (1911-1995), GER (NEPTUN KREFELD)
200 yd through 400 m breast (1934-37)
Olympics (1):
Berlin 1936: 200 m breast (2nd, 3:04.2)
World Records (2):
200 yd breast (2:44.9, Krefeld, 1935, 25 m)
400 m breast (6:19.2, Copenhagen, 1937, 25 m)
European Championships (1)
Magdeburg 1934: 200 m breast (1st, 3:09.1)
National Titles (3):
200 m breast (1934-36)

GERAGHTY, AGNES (1907-1974), USA (WOMEN'S SA)
100 yd through 400 m breast (1924-30)
Olympics (2):
Paris 1924: 200 m breast (2nd, 3:34.0)
Amsterdam 1928: 200 m breast (eliminated in semi, no time; 3:18.8 in heat)
World Records (2):
100 m breast (1:28.8, St. Augustine, 1926, 25 yd)
400 m breast (7:04.8, Portsmouth, 1925, 40 yd)
National Titles (NAAU Outdoor) (6):
220 yd breast (1924-29)
National Titles (NAAU Indoor) (5):
100 yd breast (1926-27, 30), 220 yd breast (1924-25)

GLANCY, HARRISON "HARRY" (1904-2002), USA (CINCI Y, PITTS. AA, PENN AC)
200 m free through mile, 300 through 330 yd IM (1923-28)
Olympics (2):
Paris 1924: 4 x 200 m free relay (1st, 9:53.4)
Amsterdam 1928: did not start
National Titles (NAAU Outdoor) (3):
220 yd free (2:36.6, 1923), mile free (24:27.8, 1925), 300 yd IM (4:02.4, 1925)
International Swimming Hall of Fame (1990)

GUEST, IRENE (1900-1979), USA (MEADOWBROOK CLUB)
100 m through 220 yd free (1920-21)
Olympics (1):
Antwerp 1920: 100 m free (2nd, 1:17.0), 4 x 100 m free relay (1st, 5:11.6)
International Swimming Hall of Fame (1990)

HAINLE, MAX (1882-1961), GER (STUTTGARTER ASC)
200 through 1500 m free (1897-1900)
Olympics (1):
Paris 1900: 200 m team swim (1st, no time), 1000 m free (4th, 15:22.0)

HUSZAGH, KENNETH (1891-1950), USA (CHICAGO AA, NORTHWESTERN UNIV.)
50 through 220 yd free (1911-12)
Olympics (1):
  Stockholm 1912: 100 m free (3rd, 1:05.6), 4 x 200 m free relay (2nd, 10:20.2)

HVEGER, RAGNHILD (1920-   ), DEN (HS)
100 m free through mile, 100 through 400 m back (1935-54)
Olympics (2):
  Berlin 1936: 100 m free (eliminated in semi, 1:14.0), 400 m free (2nd, 5:27.5), 4 x 100 m free relay (7th, 4:51.4)
  Helsinki 1952: 100 m free (eliminated in semi, 1:08.2), 400 m free (5th, 5:16.9), 4 x 100 m free relay (4th, 4:36.2, 4th leg, 1:07.0)
World Records (36):
  100 yd free (59.7, Aarhus, 1939, 25 m)
  200 m free (2:2:21.7, Aarhus, 1938, 25 m)
  220 yd free (2:22.6, Copenhagen, 1939, 25 yd)
  300 yd free (3:25.6, Copenhagen, 1938, 25 yd)
  300 m free (3:51.1, Copenhagen, 1937, 25 m; 3:48.8, Copenhagen, 1938, 25 m; 3:46.9, Copenhagen, 1938, 25 m; 3:42.5, Copenhagen, 1940, 25 m)
  400 m free (5:14.2, Copenhagen, 1937, 25 m; 5:14.0, Gand, 1937, 25 m; 5:12.4, Magdeburg, 1937, 25 m; 5:11.0, Copenhagen, 1937, 25 m; 5:08.2, Copenhagen,1938, 25 m; 5:06.1, Copenhagen, 1938, 25 m; 5:05.4, Svenborg, 1940, 25 m; 5:00.1, Copenhagen, 1940, 25 m)
  440 yd free (5:12.8, Copenhagen, 1937, 25 m; 5:11.5, Copenhagen, 1942, 25 m)
  500 yd free (6:14.8, Copenhagen, 1936, 25 m; 5:37.9, Aarhus, 1937, 25 m; 5:53.0, Copenhagen, 1942, 25 m)
  500 m free (6:45.7, Copenhagen, 1936, 25 m)
  800 m free (11:11.7s, Copenhagen, 1936, 50 m; 10:52.5s, Copenhagen, 1941, 50 m)
  880 yd free (11:16.1, Stockholm, 1937, 50 m; 11:08.7s, Copenhagen, 1941, 50 m)
  1000 yd free (12:36.0, Helsingor, 1938, 50 m)
  1000 m free (14:35.6s, Helsingor, 1936, 50 m; 14:12.3, Stockholm, 1937, 50 m; 14:09.2s, Helsingor, 1940, 50 m; 13:54.4s, Copenhagen, 1941, 50 m)
  1500 m free (21:45.7s, Helsingor, 1938, 50 m; 21:10.1s, Helsingor, 1940, 50 m; 20:57.0s, Copenhagen, 1941, 50 m)
  Mile free (23:11.5s, Helsingor, 1938, 50 m)
  200 m back (2:41.3, Aarhus, 1937, 25 m)
World Long Course Best Times (20):
  200 m free (2:29.4s, Helsingor, 1937; 2:27.5s, Copenhagen, 1937)
  400 m free (5:23.3, Stockholm, 1937; 5:20.6, Budapest, 1938; 5:16.8s, Sonderstrand, 1938; 5:13.9s, Sonderstrand, 1938; 5:09.7, London, 1938)
  800 m free (11:11.7s, Copenhagen, 1936; 10:52.5s, Copenhagen, 1941)
  880 yd free (11:16.1, Stockholm, 1937; 11:08.7s, Copenhagen, 1941)
  1000 yd free (12:36.0, Helsingor, 1938)
  1000 m free (14:35.6s, Helsingor, 1936; 14:12.3, Stockholm, 1937; 14:09.2s, Helsingor, 1940; 13:54.4s, Copenhagen, 1941)
  1500 m free (21:45.7s, Helsingor, 1938; 21:10.1s, Helsingor, 1940; 20:57.0s, Copenhagen, 1941)
  Mile free (23:11.5s, Helsingor, 1938)
European Championships (2):
  London 1938: 100 m free (1st, 1:06.2), 400 m free (1st, 5:09.0), 4 x 100 m free relay (1st, 4:31.6)
  Torino 1954: 100 m free (5th, 1:08.7), 400 m free (eliminated in heat, 5:36.9), 4 x 100 m free relay (4th, 4:38.5, 4th leg, 1:08.0)
National Titles (17):
  100 m free (1936-42), 400 m free (1935-42), 100 m back (1937-38)
International Swimming Hall of Fame (1966)

IRIYE, TOSHIO (1911-   ), JPN (IBARAGI, WASEDA UNIV.)
100 through 400 m back (1927-34)
Olympics (2):
Amsterdam 1928: 100 m back (4th, 1:13.6)
Los Angeles 1932: 100 m back (2nd, 1:09.8)
World Records (2):
200 m back (2:37.8, Tamagawa, 1928)
400 m back (5:42.0, Wakayama, 1928, 25 m)
National Titles (2):
100 and 200 m back (1928)
University Titles (3):
100 m back (1929-31)

JACOBSEN, ELSE (1911-1965), DEN (DKG)
100 and 200 m breast (1927-34)
Olympics (2):
Amsterdam 1928: 200 m breast (4th, 3:19.0)
Los Angeles 1932: 200 m breast (3rd, 3:07.4)
World Records (6):
100 m breast (1:26.2, Copenhagen, 1932, 33.3 m; 1:26.0, Stockholm, 1932, 25 m)
200 yd breast (2:50.4, Copenhagen, 1932, 33.3 m; 2:49.5, Stockholm, 1933, 25 yd)
200 m breast (3:16.6, Oslo, 1927, 50 m; 3:03.4, Stockholm, 1932, 25 yd)
World Long Course Best Times (1):
200 m breast (3:16.6, Oslo, 1927)
European Championships (1):
Magdeburg 1934: 200 m breast (tie for 5th, 3:16.4)
National Titles (8): 200 m breast (1927-34)

JARVIS, JOHN (1872-1933), ENG (LEICESTER SC)
400 through 4000 m free (1897-1908)
Olympics (2):
Paris 1900: 1000 m free (1st, 13:40.2), 4000 m free (1st, 58:24.0), 5 x 400 m free relay (3rd, no time)
London 1908: 1500 m free (dropped out of semi)
Interim Games (1):
Athens 1906: 400 m free (3rd, no time)
English ASA Titles (23):
440 yd free (1898, 1900), 500 yd free (1898-01), 880 yd free (1989-01), mile free (1898-02), long distance (1898-04, 06)
International Swimming Hall of Fame (1968)

JULIN, HARALD (1890-1967), SWE (SKK)
100 m free, 100 m back, 200 m breast (1908-17)
Olympics (2):
London 1908: 100 m free (3rd, 1:08.0)
Stockholm 1912: 100 m free (eliminated in heat, 1:11.8), 200 m breast (eliminated in semi, 3:10.6)
National Titles (13):
100 m free (1907-09, 11, 13), 100 m back (1910-14, 16-17), 200 m breast (1910)

KAHANAMOKU, DUKE (1890-1968), USA (HUI NALU)
100 through 440 yd free (1911-24)
Olympics (3):
Stockholm 1912: 100 m free (1st, 1:03.4), 4 x 200 m free relay (2nd, 10:20.2)

Antwerp 1920: 100 m free (1st, 1:01.4), 4 x 200 m free relay (1st, 10:04.4)
Paris 1924: 100 m free (2nd, 1:01.4)
World Records (7):
   100 yd free (54.6, San Francisco, 1913, 100 yd; 53.8, Sydney, 1915, 100 yd; 53.2, Honolulu, 1915, 100 yd; 53.0, Honolulu, 1917, 100 yd)
   100 m free (1:01.6, Hamburg, 1912, 100 m; 1:01.4, New York, 1918, 100 m; 1:00.4, Antwerp, 1920, 100 m)
National Titles (NAAU Outdoor) (3):
   100 yd free (53.2, 1916; 54.0, 1917; 55.4, 1920)
National Titles (NAAU Indoor) (2):
   50 yd free (23.8, 1916), 100 yd free (57.8, 1912)
International Swimming Hall of Fame (1965)

KAHANAMOKU, SAMUEL (1904-?), USA (HUI NALU)
100 yd and 100 m free (1924-25)
Olympics (1):
   Paris 1924: 100 m free (3rd, 1:01.8)

KAWAISHI, TATSUGO (1911-   ), JPN (KEIO UNIV.)
50 and 100 m free (1931-32)
Olympics (1):
   Los Angeles 1932: 100 m free (2nd, 58.6)
KAWATSU, KENTARU (1914-1970), JPN (MEIJI UNIV.)
100 through 400 m back (1930-35)
Olympics (1):
   Los Angeles 1932: 100 m back (3rd, 1:10.0)
World Records (1):
   400 m back (5:37.8, Tokyo, 1933, 25 m)
National Titles (1):
   100 m back (1931)
University Titles (3):
   100 m back (1932-34)

KEALOHA, PUA (1902-1973), USA (HUI MAKANI)
100 and 200 m free (1920-21)
Olympics (1):
   Antwerp 1920: 100 m free (2nd, 1:02.2), 4 x 200 m free relay (1st, 10:04.4)
National Titles (NAAU Outdoor) (1):
   100 yd free (53.0, 1921)

KEALOHA, WARREN (1903-1972), USA (HUI MAKANI)
50 yd free and 100 m through 150 yd back (1920-26)
Olympics (2):
   Antwerp 1920: 100 m back (1st, 1:15.2)
   Paris 1924: 100 m back (1st, 1:13.2)
World Records (5):
   100 m back (1:14.8, Antwerp, 1920, 100 m; 1:12.8, Honolulu, 1922, 25 yd; 1:12.4, Honolulu, 1924, 50 m; 1:11.4, Honolulu, 1926, 25 yd)
   150 yd back (1:44.8, Honolulu, 1923, 25 yd)
National Titles (NAAU Outdoor) (1):
   150 yd back (1:49.0, 1921)
National Titles (NAAU Indoor) (2):
   50 yd free (25.0, 1921; 23.6, 1922)
International Swimming Hall of Fame (1968)

KELLNER, PAUL (1891-1972), GER (BERLIN)
100 and 200 m back (1911-13)
Olympics (1):
 Stockholm 1912: 100 m back (3rd, 1:24.0)

KEMP, PETER (? - ?), ENG
Olympics (1):
 Paris 1900: 200 m obstacle race (3rd, 2:47.4)

KEGERIS, RAYMOND (1901-1975), USA (LAAC)
100 m and 150 yd back (1920-22)
Olympics (1):
 Antwerp 1920: 100 m back (2nd, 1:16.2)
National Titles (NAAU Indoor) (2):
 150 yd back (1:49.8, 1921; 1:49.8, 1922)

**KIEFER, ADOLPH (1918-), USA (LAKE SHORE AC, MEDINAH CLUB, CHICAGO TOW-
ERS, USNR BAINBRIDGE)**
100 through 220 yd free, 100 yd through 400 m back, 300 through 330 yd IM (1935-45)
Olympics (1):
 Berlin 1936: 100 m back (1st, 1:05.9)
World Records (17):
 100 yd back (58.8, Columbus, 1939, 25 yd; 57.8, Cincinnati, 1941, 25 yd; 56.8, Annapolis,
 1944, 25 yd)
 100 m back (1:07.0, Berlin, 1935, 25 m; 1:06.2, Krefeld, 1935, 25 m; 1:04.9, Breslau, 1935,
 25 m; 1:04.8, Detroit, 1936, 25 yd)
 150 yd back (1:35.6, Chicago, 1935, 25 yd; 1:33.9, Aarhus, 1935, 25 yd; 1:32.7, Chicago, 1936,
 25 yd; 1:30.4, Honolulu, 1941)
 200 m back (2:24.0, Chicago, 1935, 25 yd; 2:23.0, Honolulu, 1941, 25 yd; 2:19.3, Annapolis,
 1944, 25 yd)
 400 m back (5:17.8, Chicago, 1935, 25 yd; 5:13.4, Copenhagen, 1936, 25 m; 5:10.9, Cincinnati,
 1941, 25 yd)
Pan Am Games (1):
 Guayaquil 1939: 100 m back (1st, 1:06.0), 200 m back (1st, 2:27.4), 4 x 100 m free relay (1st,
 4:02.4)
National Titles (NAAU Outdoor) (14):
 220 yd free (2:18.7, 1938), 100 yd back (1:07.8, 1935; 1:06.5, 1936; 1:06.3, 1937; 1:07.8, 1938;
 1:06.6, 1939; 1:05.5, 1940), 100 m back (1:06.3, 1941), 110 yd back (1:06.6, 1942; 1:07.0,
 1943), 330 yd IM (4:02.0, 1938; 4:02.2, 1939; 3:58.6, 1940; 4:04.5, 1943)
National Titles (NAAU Indoor) (14):
 150 yd back (1:36.1, 1935; 1:32.7, 1936; 1:33.0, 1937; 1:33.2, 1939; 1:33.3, 1940; 1:33.1, 1941;
 1:30.5, 1942; 1:31.0, 1944; 1:33.5, 1945), 300 yd IM (3:29.6, 1940; 3:29.6, 1941; 3:28.2,
 1942; 3:23.9, 1944; 3:30.4, 1945)
International Swimming Hall of Fame (1965)

KIGHT-WINGARD, LENORE (1911-2006), USA (CARNEGIE LIBRARY)
100 yd free through mile (1929-36)
Olympics (2):
 Los Angeles 1932: 400 m free (2nd, 5:28.6)
 Berlin 1936: 400 m free (3rd, 5:29.0)
World Records (6):
 300 yd free (3:38.4, Buffalo, 1933, 25 yd)
 440 yd free (5:30.0, Boston, 1934, 25 yd)
 500 yd free (6:15.2, Boston, 1934, 25 yd)

500 m free (6:50.8, Nassau, 1935, 25 yd)
800 m free (11:34.4, Manhattan Beach, 1935, 55 yd)
880 yd free (11:34.4, Manhattan Beach, 1935, 55 yd)
World Long Course Best Times (10):
400 m free (1933, 35)
800 m free (1933-36)
Mile free (1933-36)
National Titles (NAAU Outdoor) (13):
110 yd free (1931), 440 yd free (1933-36), 880 yd free (1933-36), mile free (1933-36)
National Titles (NAAU Indoor) (7):
100 yd free (1933), 220 yd free (1933-35), 500 yd free (1933-35)
International Swimming Hall of Fame (1981)

KING, ELLEN (1909-1994), SCO (EDINBURGH ZENITH SC)
100 yd and 100 m free, 100 m and 150 yd back, 200 yd breast (1924-30)
Olympics (2):
Paris 1924: 100 m back (6th, 1:38.2)
Amsterdam 1928: 100 m back (2nd, 1:22.2), 4 x 100 m free relay (2nd, 5:13.4)
World Records (2):
150 yd back (1:57.2, Southport, 1928, 25 yd)
200 yd breast (3:02.0, Glasgow, 1927, 25 yd)
European Championships (1):
Bologna 1927: 100 m back (3rd, 1:30.0), 4 x 100 m free relay (1st, 5:11.0)
Empire Games (1):
Hamilton 1930: 100 yd free (2nd, 1:07.4), 200 yd breast (3rd, no time), 4 x 100 yd free relay (3rd, 4:37.0)
English ASA Titles (6):
100 yd free (1:09.0, 1930), 150 yd back (1925-26, 28), 200 yd breast (1927-28)

KIRSCHBAUM, WILLIAM (1902-1953), USA (HUI MAKANI)
200 m breast (1924)
Olympics (1):
Paris 1924: 200 m breast (3rd, 3:01.0)

KISS, GEZA (1882-1952), HUN (MUE, MTK)
100 yd free through mile (1903-06)
Olympics (1):
St. Louis 1904: 880 yd free (3rd, no time), mile free (2nd, 28:28.2)
Interim Games (1):
Athens 1906: 4 x 250 m free relay (1st, 16:52.4)
National Titles (5):
100, 200, 400 yd and mile free (1903-06)

KITAMURA, KUSUO (1917-1996), JPN (KUICHI)
400 through 1500 m free (1931-34)
Olympics (1):
Los Angeles 1932: 1500 m free (1st, 19:12.4)
World Records (1):
1000 m free (12:42.6, Tokyo, 1933, 50 m)
National Titles (2):
1500 m free (1932-33)
International Swimming Hall of Fame (1965)

KIYOKAWA, MASAJI (1913-1999), JPN (KEIO UNIV.)
100 through 400 m back (1930-36)
Olympics (2):
   Los Angeles 1932: 100 m back (1st, 1:08.6)
   Berlin 1936: 100 m back (3rd, 1:08.4)
World Records (1):
   400 m back (5:30.4, Tokyo, 1933, 25 m)
World Long Course Best Time (1):
   200 m back (2:35.8, Tokyo, 1933)
National Titles (4):
   100 and 200 m back (1931-33)
University Titles (1):
   100 m back (1935)
International Swimming Hall of Fame (1978)

KOIKE, REIZO (1915-1998), JPN (NOMATA SHUGYU HS, KEIO UNIV.)
100 and 200 m breast (1930-38, 46)
Olympics (2):
   Los Angeles 1932: 200 m breast (2nd, 2:46.6)
   Berlin 1936: 200 m breast (3rd, 2:44.2)
World Long Course Best Times (9):
   100 m breast (1:16.0, Tokyo, 1932; 1:14.8, Tokyo, 1933; 1:13.8, Tokyo, 1934; 1:12.6, Tokyo, 1935)
   200 m breast (2:46.2, Los Angeles, 1932; 2:44.9, Los Angeles, 1932; 2:44.2, Tokyo, 1933; 2:43.0, Tokyo, 1934; 2:41.2, Tokyo, 1935)
National Titles (9):
   100 and 200 m breast (1931-34, 37, 46)
University Titles (5):
   100 and 200 m breast (1934-37)
International Swimming Hall of Fame (1996)

KOJAK, GEORGE (1910-1996), USA (BOYS CLUB OF NY, RUTGERS UNIV., NYAC)
50 through 220 yd free, 100 yd through 400 m back (1927-32)
Olympics (1):
   Amsterdam 1928: 100 m free (4th, 1:00.8), 100 m back (1st, 1:08.2), 4 x 200 m free relay (1st, 9:36.2)
World Records (8):
   100 m back (1:09.0, Detroit, 1928; 1:08.2, Amsterdam, 1928)
   150 yd back (1:38.4, St. Louis, 1929, 25 yd; 1:38.0, Cambridge, 1930, 25 yd; 1:37.4, New Haven, 1932, 25 yd)
   400 m back (5:52.2, Massapaqua, 1927, 55 yd; 5:43.3, Vienna, 1928, 33.3 m; 5:16.4, New York, 1936, 25 yd)
National Titles (NAAU Outdoor) (4):
   100 m free (59.2, 1930), 220 yd back (2:36.0, 1927; 2:37.8, 1928; 2:35.8, 1930)
National Titles (NAAU Indoor) (3):
   150 yd back (1:39.2, 1927; 1:39.0, 1929; 1:38.0, 1930)
NCAA Titles (3):
   100 yd free (52.6, 1931), 150 yd back (1:38.4, 1929; 1:38.0, 1930)
International Swimming Hall of Fame (1968)

LACKIE, ETHEL (1907-1979), USA (ILLINOIS AC)
100 through 440 yd free (1924-28)
Olympics (1):
   Paris 1924: 100 m free (1st, 1:12.4), 4 x 100 m free relay (1st, 4:58.8)

World Records (2):
100 yd free (1:00.9, Philadelphia, 1926, 25 yd)
100 m free (1:10.0, Toledo, 1926, 25 yd)
World Long Course Best Times (2):
100 m free (1924, 26)
National Titles (NAAU Outdoor) (2):
100 yd free (1924), 100 m free (1926)
National Titles (NAAU Indoor) (3):
100 yd free (1925-26, 28)
International Swimming Hall of Fame (1969)

LAMBERT, ADELAIDE (1907-1996), USA (WSA)
100 m free, 100 and 200 m back (1923-28)
Olympics (1):
Amsterdam 1928: 4 x 100 m free relay (1st, 4:47.6)
National Titles (NAAU Outdoor) (5):
100 yd free, 220 yd back, 330 yd IM (1923, 25-27)
National Titles (NAAU Indoor) (1): 300 yd IM (1927)

LANE, FRED (1877-1969), AUS (NEW SOUTH WALES, E. SYDNEY SC)
100 yd free through mile (1898-1902)
Olympics (1):
Paris 1900: 200 m free (1st, 2:25.2), 200 m obstacle race (1st, 2:38.4)
World Records (1):
220 yd free (2:28.6, Weston-Super-Mare, 1902, 33.3 yd)
National Titles (3):
100 yd free (1898, 1902), 220 yd free (1902)
New South Wales Titles (10):
100 yd free through mile free (1897-1902)
International Swimming Hall of Fame (1970)

LANGER, LUDY (1893-1984), USA (LAAC, UNIV. OF CALIFORNIA, OLYMPIC CLUB, HUI NALU)
220 yd free through mile (1915-21)
Olympics (1):
Antwerp 1920: 400 m free (2nd, 5:29.2)
World Records (2):
440 yd free (5:22.2, San Francisco, 1914, 75 yd)
500 m free (6:55.4, Adelaide, 1921, 110 yd)
National Titles (NAAU Outdoor) (8):
440 yd free (5:32.2, 1915; 5:38.6, 1916; 5:45.0, 1921), 880 yd free (12:08.6, 1915; 12:00.2, 1916; 12:03.0, 1921), mile free (24:59.4, 1915; 23:22.0, 1916)
International Swimming Hall of Fame (1988)

LAUFER, WALTER (1906-1984), USA (CINCINNATI Y, LAKE SHORE AC)
100 through 220 yd free, 100 through 220 yd back, 300 through 330 yd IM (1925-31)
Olympics (1):
Amsterdam 1928: 100 m free (5th, 1:01.0), 100 m back (2nd, 1:10.0), 4 x 200 m free relay (1st, 9:36.2, 2nd leg)
World Records (4):
100 m back (1:11.2, Berlin, 1926, 100 m)
200 m back (2:47.1, Bremen, 1926, 100 m; 2:44.9, Nurnberg, 50 m; 2:38.8, Magdeburg, 1926, 25 m)
National Titles (NAAU Outdoor) (1):

220 yd back (2:50.0, 1925)
National Titles (NAAU Indoor) (10):
   100 yd free (52.4, 1926; 51.8, 1929; 52.8, 1930), 220 yd free (2:12.8, 1929), 300 yd IM (3:45.6,
   1926; 3:39.8, 1928), 150 yd back (1:42.8, 1926; 1:37.6, 1928; 1:40.6, 1930; 1:39.9, 1931)

LEARY, SCOTT (1881-1958), USA (OLYMPIC CLUB)
50 and 100 yd free (1904)
Olympics (1):
   St. Louis 1904: 50 yd free (2nd, 28.6), 100 yd free (3rd, no time)

LUTZOW, WILHELM (1892-1916), GER (HELLAS MAGDEBURG)
100 through 400 m breast (1912-21)
Olympics (1):
   Stockholm 1912: 200 m breast (2nd, 3:05.0)
World Records (1):
   100 m breast (1:16.8, Magdeburg, 1921, 25 m)

PEDER LYKKEBERG (1878-1944), DEN (HERMES)
Underwater swim for distance and time (1900)
Olympics (1):
   Paris 1900: underwater swim for distance and time (3rd, 147.0 points)

MADISON, HELENE (1913-1970), USA (WASHINGTON AC)
100 yd free through mile (1930-32)
Olympics (1):
   Los Angeles 1932: 100 m free (1st, 1:06.8), 400 m free (1st, 5:28.5), 4 x 100 m free relay
   (1st, 4:38.0)
World Records (22):
   100 yd free (1:00.8, Miami Beach, 1930, 25 yd; 1:00.0, Boston, 1931, 25 yd)
   100 m free (1:08.0, Miami Beach, 1930, 25 yd; 1:06.6, Boston, 1931, 25 yd)
   200 m free (2:34.6, St. Augustine, 1930, 25 yd)
   220 yd free (2:35.0, Miami Beach, 1930, 25 yd; 2:34.8, Seattle, 1931, 25 yd)
   300 yd free (3:41.6, Seattle, 1930, 25 yd; 3:39.0, Seattle, 1930, 25 yd)
   300 m free (3:59.5, Seattle, 1930, 25 yd)
   400 m free (5:31.0, Seattle, 1931, 25 yd; 5:28.5, Los Angeles, 1932, 50 m)
   440 yd free (5:39.4, Long Beach, 1930, 55 yd; 5:31.0, Seattle, 1931, 25 yd)
   500 yd free (6:16.4, Miami Beach, 1930, 25 yd)
   500 m free (7:12.0, Detroit, 1931, 25 yd)
   800 m free (11:41.2, Long Beach, 1930, 55 yd)
   880 yd free (11:41.2, Long Beach, 1930, 55 yd)
   1000 yd free (13:23.6, New York, 1931, 55 yd)
   1000 m free (14:44.8, New York, 1931, 55 yd)
   1500 m free (23:17.2, New York, 1931, 55 yd)
   Mile free (24:34.6, Long Beach, 1930, 55 yd)
World Records (Relay) (1):
   4 x 100 m free relay (4:38.0, Los Angeles, 1932)
World Long Course Best Times (12):
   100 m free (1:08.2y, Long Beach, 1930, 55 yd; 1:06.8, Los Angeles, 1932)
   200 m free (2:36.4s, San Francisco, 1930)
   400 m free (5:32.4sy, Jones Beach, 1932, 55 yd; 5:28.5, Los Angeles, 1932)
   440 yd free (5:39.4s, Long Beach, 1930, 55 yd)
   800 m free (11:41.2sy, Long Beach, 1930, 55 yd)
   880 yd free (11:41.2sy, Long Beach, 1930, 55 yd)
   1000 yd free (13:23.6, New York, 1931)

1000 m free (14:44.8, New York, 1931)
1500 m free (23:17.2sy, Bronx Beach, 1931, 55 yd)
Mile free (24:34.6s, Long Beach, 1930, 55 yd)
National Titles (NAAU Outdoor) (8):
110 yd free, 440 yd free, 880 yd free, mile free (1930-31)
National Titles (NAAU Indoor) (9):
100 yd free, 220 yd free, 500 yd free (1930-32)
International Swimming Hall of Fame (1966)

MAEHATA, HIDEKO (1914-1995), JPN
100 through 500 m breast (1929-37)
Olympics (2):
Los Angeles 1932: 200 m breast (2nd, 3:06.4)
Berlin 1936: 200 m breast (1st, 3:03.6)
World Records (3):
200 m breast (3:00.4, Tokyo, 1933, 25 m)
400 m breast (6:24.8, Tokyo, 1933, 25 m)
500 m breast (8:03.8, Tokyo, 1933, 25 m)
World Long Course Best Times (7):
100 m breast (1:27.0, Tokyo, 1933; 1:26.0, Tokyo, 1933)
200 m breast (3:05.2, Tokyo, 1933; 3:04.8, Tokyo, 1935; 3:01.9, Berlin, 1936)
400 m breast (6:24.8, Tokyo, 1933, 25 m)
500 m breast (8:03.8, Tokyo, 1933, 25 m)
National Titles (7):
200 m breast (1930-36)
International Swimming Hall of Fame (1979)

MAHLISCH, KURT (1881-1970), GER (ASV BRESLAU)
200 and 400 m breast (1912)
Olympics (1):
Stockholm 1912: 200 m breast (3rd, 3:08.0), 400 m breast (4th, 6:37.0)

MAKAAL, JENNIE (1913-?), SAF
100 through 440 yd free (1932-34)
Olympics (1):
Los Angeles 1932: 100 m free (6th, 1:10.8), 400 m free (3rd, 5:47.3)
Empire Games (1):
London 1934: 440 yd free (2nd, 5:53.0), 4 x 100 yd free relay (2nd, 4:34.0)

MAKINO, SHOZO (1915-1987), JPN (MUTUKE HS, WASEDA UNIV.)
400 through 1500 m free (1929-38)
Olympics (2):
Los Angeles 1932: 1500 m free (2nd, 19:14.1)
Berlin 1936: 400 m free (3rd, 4:48.1)
World Records and World Long Course Best Times (5):
400 m free (4:46.8, Tokyo, 1935)
800 m free (10:16.6, Osaka, 1931; 10:08.6, Tokyo, 1933; 10:01.2, Tokyo, 1933; 9:55.8, Tokyo, 1934)
National Titles (3):
400 and 1500 m free (1930, 33)
University Titles (4):
400 and 800 m free (1934-35, 37)
International Swimming Hall of Fame (1991)

MALMROTH, HAKAN (1900-1987), SWE (OREBRO SS)
100 through 400 m breast (1918-22)
Olympics (1):
Antwerp 1920: 200 m breast (1st, 3:04.4), 400 m breast (1st, 6:31.0)
National Titles (5):
200 m breast (1918, 22), 400 m breast (1918-19, 22)
International Swimming Hall of Fame (1980)

MARTIN, LOUIS (? - ?), FRA (PN LILLE)
400 through 4000 m free (1900)
Olympics (1):
Paris 1900: 1000 m free (5th, 16:30.4), 4000 m free (3rd, 1:13:08.4)
National Titles (1):
400 m ocean swim (1900)

MASTENBROEK, HENDRIKA "RIE" (1919-2003), NED (ODZ)
100 through 400 m free, 100 and 200 m back (1933-37)
Olympics (1):
Berlin 1936: 100 m free (1st, 1:05.9), 400 m free (1st, 5:26.4), 100 m back (2nd, 1:19.2),
    4 x 100 m free relay (1st, 4:36.0)
World Records (6):
100 m back (1:16.8, Dusseldorf, 1934, 25 m; 1:15.8, Amsterdam, 1936, 25 m)
200 m back (2:49.6, Amsterdam, 1935, 25 m)
400 m back (6:05.0, Basel, 1935, 25 m; 5:59.8, Copenhagen, 1936, 25 m; 5:48.8, Rotterdam,
    1936, 25 m)
World Records (Relay) (2):
4 x 100 m free relay (4:33.3, Rotterdam, 1934, 25 m; 4:32.8, Rotterdam, 1936, 25 m)
World Long Course Best Times (2):
400 m free (5:27.4, Rotterdam, 1934; 5:26.4, Berlin, 1936)
World Long Course Best Times (Relay) (1):
4 x 100 m free relay (4:36.0, Berlin, 1936)
European Championships (1):
Magdeburg 1934: 100 m free (2nd, 1:08.1), 400 m free (1st, 5:27.4), 100 m back (1st, 1:20.3),
    4 x 100 m free relay (1st, 4:41.5)
National Titles (4):
100 m free, 400 m free, 100 m back (1934-36)
International Swimming Hall of Fame (1968)

McGILLIVRAY, PERRY (1893-1944), USA (ILL. AC, GREAT LAKES NTS)
50 through 440 yd free, 100 m through 150 yd back (1911-20)
Olympics (2):
Stockholm 1912: 100 m free (eliminated in semi, 1:06.2), 4 x 200 m free relay (2nd, 10:20.2)
Antwerp 1920: 100 m back (4th, 1:19.4), 4 x 200 m free relay (1st, 10:04.4)
World Record (1):
150 yd back (1:48.8, Detroit, 1918, 25 yd)
National Titles (NAAU Outdoor) (2):
100 yd free (56.2, 1918), 110 yd free (1:05.8, 1919)
National Titles (NAAU Indoor) (14):
50 yd free (24.2, 1913; 24.4, 1915; 24.2, 1917; 24.8, 1918; 24.0, 1919), 100 yd free (56.2, 1916;
    55.4, 1918; 55.4, 1919), 220 yd free (2:34.2, 1912; 2:29.0, 1913; 2:26.6, 1915), 500 yd free
    (6:20.6, 1913), 150 yd back (1:49.6, 1918; 1:48.8, 1920)
International Swimming Hall of Fame (1981)

McKIM, JOSEPHINE (1910-1992), USA (CARNEGIE LIBRARY, LAAC)
100 yd free through mile (1928-32)
Olympics (2):
Amsterdam 1928: 400 m free (3rd, 6:00.2), 4 x 100 m free relay (in heat, 4:55.6)
Los Angeles 1932: 100 m free (4th, 1:09.3), 4 x 100 m free relay (1st, 4:38.0)
World Records (4):
300 yd free (3:49.0, Miami, 1930, 25 yd)
440 yd free (5:47.4, Honolulu, 1929, 55 yd)
800 m free (12:03.8, Honolulu, 1929, 55 yd)
880 yd free (12:03.8, Honolulu, 1929, 55 yd)
World Records (Relay) (1):
4 x 100 m free relay (4:38.0, Los Angeles, 1932)
National Titles (NAAU Outdoor) (4):
440 yd free (1929), 880 yd free (1929), mile free (1928-29)
International Swimming Hall of Fame (1991)

MEALING, PHYLLIS "BONNIE" (1912-2002), AUS (NEW SOUTH WALES, CLOVELLY, COOGEE)
100 m back (1930-35)
Olympics (1):
Los Angeles 1932: 100 m back (2nd, 1:21.3)
World Records (2):
100 m back (1:20.6, Sydney, 1930, 50 yd)
150 yd back (1:55.2, Sydney, 1930, 55 yd)
World Long Course Best Times (1):
100 m back (1:20.6, 1930)
New South Wales Titles (3):
100 yd back (1933-35)

MEDICA, JACK (1914-1985), USA (WASH. AC, UNIV. OF WASHINGTON, NYAC)
200 m free through mile (1932-39)
Olympics (1):
Berlin 1936: 400 m free (1st, 4:44.5), 1500 m free (2nd, 19:34.0), 4 x 200 m free relay (2nd, 9:03.0, 4th leg, 2:15.5)
World Records (12):
200 m free (2:07.2, Chicago, 1935, 25 yd)
220 yd free (2:07.9, Chicago, 1935, 25 yd)
300 yd free (3:04.4, Chicago, 1935, 25 yd)
300 m free (3:21.6, Chicago, 1935, 25 yd)
400 m free (4:38.7, Honolulu, 1934, 25 yd)
440 yd free (4:40.8, Honolulu, 1934, 25 yd)
500 yd free (5:26.6, Seattle, 1933, 25 yd; 5:16.3, 1935, 25 yd)
500 m free (5:57.8, 1933, 25 yd)
880 yd free (10:15.4, Chicago, 1933, 55 yd)
1000 yd free (no time, Portland, 1933, 55 yd)
Mile free (no time, Chicago, 1934, 55 yd)
USA vs Japan (1):
Tokyo 1935: 400 m free (1st, 4:45.2), 800 m free (2nd, 10:02.4), 1500 m free (4th, 19:35.8), 4 x 200 m free relay (2nd, 8:58.6, 4th leg, 2:16.0)
National Titles (NAAU Outdoor) (5):
440 yd free (4:52.8, 1933; 4:50.9, 1934), 880 yd free (10:20.4, 1933; 10:16.1, 1934), mile free (20:57.8, 1934)
National Titles (NAAU Indoor) (7):
220 yd free (2:10.8, 1935; 2:16.6, 1936; 2:12.9, 1939), 500 yd free (5:29.0, 1934; 5:16.8, 1935;

5:21.5, 1936), 1500 m free (19:06.8, 1936)
NCAA Titles (9):
220 yd free (2:13.2, 1934; 2:11.5, 1935; 2:09.6, 1936), 440 yd free (4:46.8, 1934; 4:42.5, 1935; 4:44.6, 1936), 1500 m free (19:12.1, 1934; 18:59.3, 1935; 20:23.7, 1936, 50 m)
International Swimming Hall of Fame (1966)

MIYAZAKI, YASUJI (1916-1989), JPN (HAMMATSU MS, NIHON UNIV.)
100 and 200 m free (1931-35)
Olympics (1):
Los Angeles 1932: 100 m free (1st, 58.2), 4 x 200 m free relay (1st, 8:58.4, 1st leg, 2:14.0)
National Titles (1):
100 m free (1931)
International Swimming Hall of Fame (1981)

MORTON, LUCY (1898-1980), ENG (BLACKPOOL SC)
100 and 150 yd back, 200 yd and 200 m breast (1916-24)
Olympics (1):
Paris 1924: 200 m breast (1st, 3:33.2, 3:29.4 in heat)
World Records (3):
150 yd back (2:17.0, Seacombe, 1916, 25 yd)
200 yd breast (3:11.4, Liverpool, 1916, 25 yd; 3:06.0, Blackpool, 1920, 25 yd)
English ASA Titles (2):
150 yd back (1920), 200 yd breast (1920)
International Swimming Hall of Fame (1988)

MUHE, LOTTE (1910-1981), GER (HILDESHEIM '99)
100 and 200 m breast (1927-29)
Olympics (1):
Amsterdam 1928: 200 m breast (3rd, 3:17.6)
World Records (3):
100 m breast (1:26.3, Magdeburg, 1928, 25 m)
200 m breast (3:15.8, Magdeburg, 1928, 25 m; 3:11.2, Berlin, 1928, 50 m)
European Championships (1):
Bologna 1927: 200 m breast (2nd, 3:25.2)
National Titles (2):
200 m breast (1928-29)

NEUMANN, PAUL (1877-1932), AUT (CHICAGO AA)
440 yd free through mile (1896-98)
Olympics (1):
Athens 1896: 500 m free (1st, 8:12.6)
USA National Titles (NAAU Outdoor) (3):
440 and 880 yd free, mile free (1897-98)
International Swimming Hall of Fame (1986)

NORELIUS, MARTHA (1910-1955), USA (WOMEN'S SA)
100 yd free through mile (1924-28)
Olympics (2):
Paris 1924: 400 m free (1st, 6:02.2)
Amsterdam 1928: 400 m free (1st, 5:42.8), 4 x 100 m free relay (1st, 4:47.6)
World Records (18):
200 m free (2:40.6, Miami, 1926, 25 yd)
220 yd free (2:40.6, Miami, 1926, 25 yd)
300 m free (4:08.3, Vienna, 1928, 33.3 m)

Berlin 1936: 200 m breast (2nd, 2:42.9)
World Records (1):
200 m breast (2:42.4, Dusseldorf, 1935, 25 m)
European Championships (3):
Paris 1931: 200 m breast (3rd, 2:55.0)
Magdeburg 1934: 200 m breast (1st, 2:49.0)
London 1938: 200 m breast (2nd, 2:45.9)
National Titles (5):
200 m breast (1929, 32-34, 37)
International Swimming Hall of Fame (1992)
SIX, ANDRE (? - ?), FRA
Underwater swim for distance and time (1900)
Olympics (1):
Paris 1900: underwater swim for distance and time (2nd, 185.4 points)

SKELTON, ROBERT "BOB" (1903-1977), USA (ILL. AC)
200 m through 440 yd breast (1921-26)
Olympics (1):
Paris 1924: 200 m breast (1st, 2:56.6)
World Records (1):
200 m breast (2:52.6, Milwaukee, 1924, 25 yd)
National Titles (NAAU Outdoor) (4):
220 yd breast (3:22.8, 1922; 3:06.6, 1923), 440 yd breast (6:50.4, 1921; 6:30.4, 1925)
National Titles (NAAU Indoor) (2):
220 yd breast (3:02.6, 1921; 2:58.6, 1923)
International Swimming Hall of Fame (1988)

SORENSEN, INGEBORG "INGE" (1924-   ), DEN (DKG, AFG)
100 through 500 m breast (1936-45)
Olympics (1):
Berlin 1936: 200 m breast (3rd, 3:07.8)
World Records (2):
400 m breast (6:16.2, Copenhagen, 1939, 25 m)
500 m breast (8:01.9, Copenhagen, 1937, 25 m)
European Championships (1):
London 1938: 200 m breast (1st, 3:05.4)
National Titles (10):
200 m breast (1936-45)

TAGUCHI, SHOJI (1916-   ), JPN (KYOTO, RIKKYO UNIV.)
100 and 200 m free (1934-38)
Olympics (1):
Berlin 1936: 100 m free (4th, 58.1), 4 x 200 m free relay (1st, 8:51.5, 3rd leg, 2:13.2)
World Records (Relay) (1):
4 x 200 m free relay (8:51.5, Berlin, 1936, 3rd leg, 2:13.2)
International Swimming Hall of Fame (1987)

TAKAISHI, KATSUO (1906-1966), JPN (IBARAGI, WASEDA UNIV.)
100 through 1500 m free (1923-31)
Olympics (2):
Paris 1924: 100 m free (5th, 1:03.0), 1500 m free (5th, 22:10.4), 4 x 200 m free relay (4th, 10:15.2)
Amsterdam 1928: 100 m free (3rd, 1:00.0), 400 m free (eliminated in semi, 5:10.4), 1500 m free (eliminated in semi, 21:20.7), 4 x 200 m free relay (2nd, 9:41.4)

World Long Course Best Times (1):
  50 m free (26.8, Tokyo, 1925)
National Titles (4):
  100, 200 and 400 m free (1925-27, 30)
University Titles (13):
  100 through 800 m free (1924-29, 31)
International Swimming Hall of Fame (1991)

TARIS, JEAN (1909-1977), FRA (SCUF, FFN, CNP)
100 through 1500 m free (1927-36)
Olympics (3):
  Amsterdam 1928: 1500 m free (eliminated in heat, no time), 4 x 200 m free relay (swam in heat, 10:31.4)
  Los Angeles 1932: 400 m free (2nd, 4:48.5), 1500 m free (6th, 20:09.7)
  Berlin 1936: 400 m free (6th, 4:53.8), 4 x 200 m free relay (4th, 9:18.2)
World Records (7):
  300 m free (3:27.6, Reims, 1932)
  400 m free (4:47.0, Paris, 131, 33-1/3 yd)
  500 m free (6:01.2, Reims, 1932, 25 m)
  800 m free (10:19.6, Pris, 1930; 10:17.2, Cannes, 1931; 10:15.6, Cannes, 1932)
  1000 m free (12:57.6, Paris, 1932)
European Championships (3):
  Bologna 1927: 400 m free (eliminated in heat, 5:46.0), 1500 m free (eliminated in heat, 22:49.6), 4 x 200 m free relay (eliminated in heat, 10:34.8)
  Paris 1931: 400 m free (2nd, 5:04.2), 1500 m free (4th, 21:13.8), 4 x 200 m free relay (4th, 9:59.4)
  Magdeburg 1934: 400 m free (1st, 4:55.5), 1500 m free (1st, 20:01.5), 4 x 200 m free relay (4th, 9:45.9)
National Titles (33):
  100 m free (1929-34), 200 m free (1927, 29-36), 400 m free (1927, 29-36), 1500 m free (1927, 29-30, 33-34), long distance (1933-36)
International Swimming Hall of Fame (1984)

TAYLOR, HENRY (1885-1951), ENG (HYDE SEAL ASC)
200 m free through mile (1906-12)
Olympics (3):
  London 1908: 400 m free (1st , 5:36.8), 1500 m free (1st, 22:48.40), 4 x 200 m free relay (1st, 10:55.6)
  Stockholm 1912: 400 m free (eliminated in semi, 5:48.2), 1500 m free (eliminated in semi, 24:06.4), 4 x 200 m free relay (3rd, 10:28.2)
  Antwerp 1920: 400 m free (eliminated in heat, 6:01.2), 4 x 200 m free relay (3rd, 10:37.2)
Interim Games (1):
  Athens 1906: 400 m free (2nd, 6:24.4), 4 x 300 m free relay (3rd, no time)
World Records (4):
  400 m free (5:36.8, London, 1908, 100 m)
  800 m free (11:25.4, Runcorn, 1906, 220 yd)
  880 yd free (11:25.4, Runcorn, 1906, 220 yd)
  1500 m free (22:48.4, London, 1908, 100 m)
English ASA Titles (14):
  440 yd free (1906-07), 500 yd free (1906-08, 11), 880 yd free (1906-07, 11), mile free (1906-07, 11), long distance (1909, 12, 20)
International Swimming Hall of Fame (1969)

TAYLOR, JOHN "JACK" (1931-   ), USA (FIRESTONE CLUB, OHIO ST. UNIV.)
400 through 1500 m free, 100 through 150 yd back (1948-52)
Olympics (1):
Helsinki 1952: 100 m back (3rd, 1:06.4)
World Records (1):
100 yd back (56.5, Columbus, 1951, 25 yd)
National Titles (NAAU Outdoor) (1):
1500 m free (19:48.1, 1948)
National Titles (NAAU Indoor) (3):
1500 m free (20:08.2, New Haven, 1948, 50 m), 100 yd back (58.5, 1951), 150 yd back (1:32.5, 1951)
NCAA Titles (4):
1500 m free (18:38.3, 1950), 100 yd back (57.3, 1952), 150 yd back (1:32.1, 1950), 200 yd back (2:07.3, 1951)

TERADA, NOBORU (1917-?), JPN (MITSUKE HS, KEIO UNIV.)
400 through 1500 m free (1934-38)
Olympics (1):
Berlin 1936: 1500 m free (1st, 19:13.7)
University Titles (1):
800 m free (1937)
International Swimming Hall of Fame (1994)

TSURUTA, YOSHIYUKI (1903-1986), JPN (SASEBO)
100 and 200 m breast (1925-32)
Olympics (2):
Amsterdam 1928: 200 m breast (1st, 2:48.8)
Los Angeles 1932: 200 m breast (1st, 2:45.4)
World Records (1):
200 m breast (2:45.0, Kyoto, 1927, 25 m)
World Long Course Best Times (6):
100 m breast (1:18.0, Shiba, 1929; 1:17.4, Tokyo, 1930; 1:16.6, Tokyo, 1931)
200 m breast (2:50.0, Amsterdam, 1928; 2:48.8, Amsterdam, 1928; 2:45.4, Los Angeles, 1932)
National Titles (11):
100 and 200 m breast (1925-31)
International Swimming Hall of Fame (1968)

UTO, SHUMPEI (1918-   ), JPN (RIKKYO UNIV.)
400 through 1500 m free (1934-37)
Olympics (1):
Berlin 1936: 400 m free (2nd, 4:45.6), 1500 m free (3rd, 19:34.5)
National Titles (2):
400 and 1500 m free (1936)

VERNOT, GEORGES (1901-1962), CAN (MONTREAL SC)
220 yd free through mile (1920-24)
Olympics (2):
Antwerp 1920: 400 m free (3rd, 5:29.8), 1500 m free (2nd, 22:36.4)
Paris 1924: 400 m free (eliminated in semi, 5:38.0), 1500 m free (eliminated in semi, 23:02.4)
National Titles:
220 yd free through mile (1920-24)

WAHLE, OTTO (1880-1963), AUT (WSK, NYAC)
100 m free through mile (1897-1904)

Olympics (2):
  Paris 1900: 200 m free (4th, no time), 1000 m free (2nd, 14:53.4), 200 m obstacle race (2nd, 2:40.0)
  St. Louis 1904: 440 yd free (3rd, 6:39.0), 880 yd free (4th, no time), mile free (4th, no time)
National Titles (2):
  100 m free (1896, 1899)
German National Titles (1):
  100 m free (1:23.0, Vienna, 1897)
USA Olympic Coach and Manager:
  1912 and 1920
International Swimming Hall of Fame (1996)

WAINWRIGHT, HELEN (1906-1978), USA (WOMEN'S SA)
50 yd free through mile (1921-25)
Olympics (1):
  Paris 1924: 400 m free (2nd, 6:03.8)
World Records (4):
  300 m free (4:29.8, Indianapolis, 1922, 100 yd; 4:19.4, Miami, 1924, 25 m)
  1000 yd free (14:58.4, Manhattan Beach, 1922, 110 yd)
  1500 m free (25:06.6, Manhattan Beach, 1922, 110 yd)
World Long Course Best Times (3):
  800 m free (1922)
  1500 m free (1922)
  Mile free (1922)
National Titles (NAAU Outdoor) (4):
  50 yd free (1922), 440 yd free (1924), 880 yd free (1922), mile free (1922)
National Titles (NAAU Indoor) (8):
  50 yd free (1922-23), 100 yd free (1923-24), 220 yd free (1922, 25), 500 yd free (1922, 24)
International Swimming Hall of Fame (1972)

WEHSELAU, MATIECHEN (1906-?), USA (OUTRIGGER CANOE CLUB)
100 yd and 100 m free (1921-26)
Olympics (1):
  Paris 1924: 100 m free (2nd, 1:12.8), 4 x 100 m free relay (1st, 4:58.8)
World Records (2):
  100 yd free (1:03.0, Maui, 1923, 25 yd)
  100 m free (1:12.2, Paris, 1924)
International Swimming Hall of Fame (1989)

WEISSMULLER, JOHN "JOHNNY" (1904-1984), USA (ILL. AC)
50 through 880 yd free, 100 through 150 yd back (1921-28)
Olympics (2):
  Paris 1924: 100 m free (1st, 59.0), 400 m free (1st, 5:04.2), 4 x 200 m free relay (1st, 9:53.4, 4th leg)
  Amsterdam 1928: 100 m free (1st, 58.6), 4 x 200 m free relay (1st, 9:36.2, 4th leg)
World Records (25):
  100 yd free (52.6, Honolulu, 1922, 25 yd; 52.4, Miami, 1924, 25 m; 52.2, San Francisco, 1925, 50 yd; 52.0, Seattle, 1925, 100 yd; 51.0, Ann Arbor, 1927, 25 yd)
  100 m free (58.6, Alameda, 1922, 100 yd; 57.4, Miami, 1924, 25 m)
  200 m free (2:15.6, Honolulu, 1922, 25 yd; 2:08.0, Ann Arbor, 1927, 25 yd)
  220 yd free (2:15.6, Honolulu, 1922, 25 yd; 2:15.2, McKeesport, 1925, 25 yd; 2:09.0, Ann Arbor, 1927, 25 yd)
  300 yd free (3:16.6, Philadelphia, 1927, 25 yd; 3:07.8, Chicago, 1927, 25 yd)
  400 m free (5:06.6, Honolulu, 1922, 100 yd; 4:57.0, New Haven, 1923, 25 yd)

440 yd free (5:07.8, Honolulu, 1922, 110 yd; 4:57.0, New Haven, 1923, 25 yd; 4:52.0,
  Honolulu, 1927, 110 yd)
500 yd free (5:47.6, Honolulu, 1922, 100 yd)
500 m free (6:24.2, Milwaukee, 1922, 25 yd)
800 m free (10:22.2, Honolulu, 1927, 110 yd)
880 yd free (10:22.2, Honolulu, 1927, 110 yd)
150 yd back (1:45.4, Milwaukee, 1927, 25 yd)
National Titles (NAAU Outdoor) (18):
50 yd free (23.2, 1921; 23.0, 1922)
100 yd free (52.0, 1922; 54.6, 1923; 52.0, 1925)
110 yd free (59.6, 1926; 58.0, 1927; 57.0, 1928)
220 yd free (2:28.0, 1921; 2:22.4, 1922)
440 yd free (5:16.4, 1922; 5:37.4, 1923; 5:22.5, 1925; 5:21.8, 1926; 4:52.0, 1927; 4:58.6, 1928)
880 yd free (11:12.0, 1925; 10:22.2, 1927)
National Titles (NAAU Indoor) (20):
50 yd free (23.6, 1923; 24.0, 1924; 23.2, 1925)
100 yd free (54.0, 1922; 54.8, 1923; 53.8, 1924; 52.2, 1925; 51.4, 1927; 50.8, 1928)
220 yd free (2:17.4, 1922; 2:22.0, 1923; 2:14.8, 1924; 2:10.8, 1927; 2:10.4, 1928)
500 yd free (5:46.8, 1922; 5:43.6, 1923; 5:50.4, 1924; 5:28.4, 1927; 5:35.0, 1928)
150 yd back (1:42.0, 1923)
International Swimming Hall of Fame (1965)

WOODBRIDGE, MARGARET (1902-1995), USA (DETROIT AC)
220 yd free through mile (1920-21)
Olympics (1):
Antwerp 1920: 300 m free (2nd, 4:42.8), 4 x 100 m free relay (1st, 5:11.6)
National Titles (NAAU Indoor) (2):
220 yd free (1921), 500 yd free (1920)
International Swimming Hall of Fame (1989)

WYATT, PAUL (1907-1970), USA (UNIONTOWN Y)
100 m through 220 yd back (1924-28)
Olympics (2):
Paris 1924: 100 m back (2nd, 1:15.4)
Amsterdam 1928: 100 m back (3rd, 1:12.0)
National Titles (NAAU Outdoor) (1):
220 yd back (2:45.8, 1926)
National Titles (NAAU Indoor) (1):
150 yd back (1:47.2, 1925)

WYLIE, WILHELMINA "MINA" (1891-1984), AUS (NEW SOUTH WALES)
100 yd and 100 m free (1912-20)
Olympics (1):
Stockholm 1912: 100 m free (2nd, 1:25.4)
International Swimming Hall of Fame (1975)

YLDEFONZO, TEOFILO (? - ?), PHI
200 m breast (1927-36)
Olympics (3):
Amsterdam 1928: 200 m breast (3rd, 2:56.4)
Los Angeles 1932: 200 m breast (3rd, 2:47.1)
Berlin 1936: 200 m breast (7th, 2:51.1)

YOKOYAMA, TAKASHI (1913-1966), JPN (K. SHUGYU HS, WASEDA UNIV.)
200 through 1500 m free (1930-34)
Olympics (1):
   Los Angeles 1932: 400 m free (3rd, 4:52.3)
National Titles (2):
   200 and 400 m free (1931)
University Titles (3):
   200, 400 and 800 m free (1932)

YUSA, MASANORI (1915-1975), JPN (TADOTSU, NIHON UNIV.)
100 and 200 m free (1931-40)
Olympics (2):
   Los Angeles 1932: 4 x 200 m free relay (1st, 8:58.4, 3rd leg, 2:14.0)
   Berlin 1936: 100 m free (2nd, 57.9), 4 x 200 m free relay (1st, 8:51.5, 1st leg, 2:13.4)
World Long Course Best Times (3):
   100 m free (57.2, Tokyo, 1935)
   200 m free (2:13.0, Tokyo, 1933; 2:11.2, Tokyo, 1935)
National Titles (5):
   100 and 200 m free (1933-34, 36)
University Titles (6):
   100 and 200 m free (1933-35)
International Swimming Hall of Fame (1992)

ZACHARIAS, GEORG (1884-1953), GER (WEISSENSEE '96)
100 yd back, 100 through 500 m breast (1904-07)
Olympics (1):
   St. Louis 1904: 100 yd back (3rd, 1:19.6), 440 yd breast (1st, 7:23.6)
World Records (2):
   400 m breast (6:53.4, Hermsdorf, 1907, 100 m)
   500 m breast (8:30.6, Berlin, 1904, 100 m)
International Swimming Hall of Fame (2002)

ZORILLA, ALBERTO (1906-1986), ARG (NYAC)
100 through 1500 m free (1924-28)
Olympics (2):
   Paris 1924: 100 m free (eliminated in heat, 1:08.2), 400 m free (eliminated in heat, 5:49.4), 4 x
      200 m free relay (eliminated in heat, 11:25.0)
   Amsterdam 1928: 100 m free (7th, 1:02.0), 400 m free (1st, 5:01.6), 1500 m free (5th, 21:13.8),
      4 x 200 m free relay (eliminated in heat)
International Swimming Hall of Fame (1976)

FINA Officers, 1908-1936

FINA Presidents
1924-1928	Erik Bergvall	SWE
1928-1932	Ernest Georges Drigny	FRA
1932-1936	Walther Binner	GER

FINA Honorary Secretaries
1908-1928	George W. Hearn	GBR
1928-1936	Dr. Leo Donath	HUN

FINA Honorary Treasurers
1908-1928	George W. Hearn	GBR
1928-1936	Dr. Leo Donath	HUN

Country Codes

ANZ	Australasia (1908-12, combined Australia and New Zealand)
ARG	Argentina
AUS	Australia
AUT	Austria
BEL	Belgium
BRA	Brazil
CAN	Canada
DEN	Denmark
FIN	Finland
FRA	France
GER	Germany
GBR	Great Britain
GRE	Greece
HUN	Hungary
JPN	Japan
NED	The Netherlands
NZL	New Zealand
PHI	Philippines
SAF	South Africa
SWE	Sweden
USA	United States of America